# The Adventures of Sherlock Holmes

and

# The Memoirs of Sherlock Holmes

SIR ARTHUR CONAN DOYLE

Guide written by

## Ron Simpson

A *Letts* EXPLORE **Literature Guide**

First published 1998

Letts Educational
Aldine House
Aldine Place
London W12 8AW
0181 740 2266

**Text** © Ron Simpson

**Typeset by** Jordan Publishing Design

**Text design** Jonathan Barnard

**Cover and text illustrations** Ivan Allen

**Design** © BPP (Letts Educational) Ltd

**Acknowledgements**

Outline answers are solely the responsibility of the author, and are not supplied or approved by the Exam Board.

**British Library Cataloguing in Publication Data**
A CIP record for this book is available from the British Library

ISBN 1 85758 866 5

Printed and bound in Great Britain

Ashford Colour Press, Gosport, Hampshire

Letts Educational is the trading name of BPP (Letts Educational) Ltd

# Contents

# ■ The Sherlock Holmes Stories: *The Adventures of Sherlock Holmes/ The Memoirs of Sherlock Holmes*

From *A Study in Scarlet* in 1887 to *The Case Book of Sherlock Holmes* in 1930, Sir Arthur Conan Doyle (1859–1930) published four novels and 56 stories about Sherlock Holmes, in addition to his writings in other fields. The stories in this guide were written in the early 1890s, following the success of two short novels: *A Study in Scarlet* and *The Sign of Four*. They owe their existence in part to the strict policy of the *Strand* magazine against serials.

When Conan Doyle began to write for the *Strand*, he had to develop the short story form for his Sherlock Holmes adventures: you will notice that, almost without exception, the stories are of similar length, no doubt to fit in with the *Strand* editorial policy. *A Scandal in Bohemia* appeared in July 1891 and, after writing over twenty stories in little more than two years, Conan Doyle, distracted by Holmes' success from his historical romances and serious writings, decided to kill him off. The result was the 23rd Sherlock Holmes story, *The Final Problem*, published in December 1893.

The outcry was enormous: Sherlock Holmes could not be allowed to die. However, it was not until 1903 that Holmes reappeared, to enjoy 27 more years of life, including his most famous full-length adventure, *The Hound of the Baskervilles*.

Sherlock Holmes has probably been used by more later authors in their own fiction than any other fictional creation. Films have placed him in many different places and periods of time (Conan Doyle never set a story later than 1914). Few fictional characters have ever been regarded as 'real' to the extent that Sherlock Holmes is: there is even a Sherlock Holmes Museum in Baker Street.

The 23 stories this guide deals with, collected in book form as *The Adventures* in 1892 and *The Memoirs* in 1894, are generally considered the finest Sherlock Holmes short stories and are the only ones that strictly fulfil the GCSE requirements for pre-twentieth-century fiction. Potential readers may find paperback editions which collect some of the same stories under different overall titles. As with all editions of short stories, a careful look at the contents page is recommended.

# ■ Who's who in the Sherlock Holmes stories

## Sherlock Holmes

By the time of these short stories Sherlock Holmes has mellowed from his first appearances in the early novels. Then described as 'the most perfect reasoning and observing machine that the world has seen', he is at first totally wrapped up in himself, feels no tender emotions, dismisses whole areas of human knowledge as irrelevant and shows a distaste for Mankind in general. This almost inhuman figure with, among other things, zero knowledge of philosophy, astronomy and politics takes cocaine to relieve the boredom of routine. This unlovely eccentric that Holmes once was is the figure described in *The Five Orange Pips*.

In the *Adventures* and *Memoirs* he is a much more appealing eccentric. The perfect reasoning machine insists on deducing the life story of everyone he meets from a mark on a shoe or hat. He is incapable of domestic routine as the opening of *The Musgrave Ritual* shows: tobacco in the slipper, cigars in the coal-scuttle, etc. He still abhors the idea of marriage, but can be gentle to his female clients, though only Irene Adler leaves a lasting impression. He is physically powerful, once a boxer of note, capable of feats of prodigious energy and stamina, but does not see the need for exertion for the sake of it, preferring to while away the time with his violin, his pipe or the agony column of *The Times* (no cocaine now, apart from a hint in the first story). Now Holmes frequently shows areas of knowledge (history and politics in particular) outside his original narrow range. Chemistry is also a particular study of his: original experiments, of course. Holmes as first created would not have been acceptable in a popular magazine. The version we encounter here has a sense of humour, a healthy appetite, a love of the dramatic and an occasional line in self-mockery; by the time of *The Yellow Face* Watson can refer to his 'easy genial way' as though it is habitual.

Above all it is the delight in his powers of deduction that defines his character. His contempt is often shown for the police for what he sees as their culpable stupidity. Holmes chooses his cases for the interest and the challenge: frequently he remarks that 'the great cases' are often the least interesting. Similarly, for such an elitist, his views of the aristocracy and even royalty are less than flattering. But Sherlock Holmes is always capable of surprising the reader with his views, whether on Board Schools or the desirability of uniting the Union Jack with the Stars and Stripes.

## Dr Watson

Dr Watson is the ideal narrator for these stories and appears in them in the role of Holmes' Boswell as well as his stalwart companion. As a narrator, his great quality is that, as Holmes says in *A Scandal in Bohemia* and repeats in different words elsewhere, 'you see, but you do not observe.' Watson's ability to perceive and describe details is as important as his inability to deduce from them what Holmes can. Beware of the assumption that Watson is stupid: he may well feel himself so alongside the great reasoning machine, but he makes the sensible deductions and assumptions of the ordinary intelligent man, thus throwing Holmes' abilities into glorious relief. As a character Watson is endlessly patient and tolerant, courageous and fair minded, an amiable and admirable man as well as the devoted recorder of Holmes' achievements. Don't forget either, that, as time passes, he gains some small successes applying Holmes' methods: his explanation of events in *The Greek Interpreter* is, Holmes concedes, 'not far from the truth'.

An interesting point about Watson concerns his place of residence. In the two earlier novels he is an ex-Army surgeon sharing rooms at 221B, Baker Street, with Sherlock Holmes, later marrying Mary Morstan. By *A Scandal in Bohemia* he has moved out and set up his own establishment in marriage and private practice. The need for him to leave his practice in the hands of an obliging fellow doctor (astonishingly obliging, in view of the success of the practice and the short notice given!) can become repetitive, so Conan Doyle often finds a reason for Watson to be back at Baker Street or simply assumes the original bachelor establishment. Remember that these were not originally published in sequence, but individually in *Strand*, so there is no real need for chronological order.

## The police

It is interesting that Conan Doyle makes little use of regular characters in these stories. Mrs Hudson, the landlady, makes only fleeting appearances and the same is true of Inspector Lestrade, first introduced in *A Study in Scarlet*. His appearances mark the low point in Holmes' attitude to the police: his mistrust of Holmes and Holmes' contempt for him are obvious. Throughout it is important that the police are not too efficient: how could the 'unofficial consulting detective' shine otherwise? Diligent officers (usually young) who co-operate with him are presented sympathetically, but even the best of them, Inspector Gregory in *Silver Blaze*, lacks the necessary imagination. The police even fail to arrest Moriarty despite Holmes' efforts. Holmes, on the other hand, is happy for the police to take credit: in *The Naval Treaty* he tells young Forbes that the police have had all the credit in 49 out of 53 cases. What he does expect is that the police defer to him and do not expect him always to stay within the law!

## The victims

The victims of the crimes (or, sometimes, the victims of non-crimes) are highly varied. Perhaps we might find three distinct types of victims, though many fall outside these categories. There are the client-victims, particularly courageous, straightforward, honest young people who come to Baker Street in perplexity. The most appealing of these characters are young women (Helen Stonor, Violet Hunter, Mary Sutherland), though Hall Pycroft takes an honourable place in the list. Most eventually come to no great harm, though John Openshaw fails to escape his fate. A second very large group is criminals who suffer rough justice: Straker killed by his horse, Captain Calhoun going down with his ship, Kemp and Latimer stabbed in Budapest and many others. A final very Victorian group consists of middle-aged men who have progressed from wild youth in the colonies or in America to become very respectable, but whose past strikes them down. Colonel Barclay and Mr Trevor die of shock; others, like Colonel Openshaw or Charles McCarthy, are murdered.

## The criminals

There are few full-time criminals in the Sherlock Holmes stories: Moriarty, the 'Napoleon of Crime', of course, and another criminal of great skill and daring, John Clay, 'a young man ... at the head of his profession', the Beddington brothers and the Worthingdon bank gang. More often, however, people act under financial pressure: several stories involve preventing marriages to gain access to money, typical of a materialistic age with strict parental control. Very often there is no criminal, or there is merely someone with a criminal past: in the latter case, as the above note indicates, criminals can turn into victims.

# Themes in the Sherlock Holmes stories

**Deduction**

## Deduction

The main enjoyment of the Sherlock Holmes stories lies in the deductive powers of Holmes. Even in the few stories where he takes little active part, we trust him to explain the mystery. He relies upon logic and fortunately the other characters behave in predictable patterns: if the logical place to put a note is in a dressing-gown, that is where it is put. The other key element is observation, which means not just seeing, but seeing what is important. Of many definitions of Holmes' method, the following comes from *The Reigate Squires*: 'It is of the highest importance in the art of detection to be able to recognise out of a number of facts which are incidental and which vital.' Holmes' virtuoso displays at the start of many of the stories (the scientific analysis of the old felt hat in *The Blue Carbuncle*, for instance, or the ruminations on Grant Munro's pipe in *The Yellow Face*) give as much pleasure as the actual solving of the mysteries.

**London**

## London

Though many of the stories move to different locations, all start in London, usually in Baker Street, and Conan Doyle's knowledge of the late nineteenth-century city is thorough and convincing. Whether in high society or seedy opium dens or anything in between, whether dealing in street plans, transport routes or character types, Conan Doyle's picture of the capital and the suburbs seems authentic. Note also the effect on the stories of London as capital of Empire. The nineteenth century was a period of colonial expansion, Victoria had recently become Empress of India, and the Holmes stories draw on murky careers in the colonies, strange foreign creatures and the trade of the gate of Empire, the Port of London, to create an exotic flavour.

**Deception**

## Deception

Deception lies at the heart of many of the stories: Clay creating the Red-Headed League, Hatherley the engineer being lured to Eyford by a spurious tale, Hall Pycroft's non-existent new job. There is also much deception by disguise. It is no coincidence that there is a story entitled *A Case of Identity*: the title could apply to several others, too. Neville St. Clair in *The Man with the Twisted Lip* is perhaps the most notably disguised character, but even a horse is liable to operate incognito! However, the character who uses deception or disguise with most relish and most skill is Sherlock Holmes himself. The proof of his excellence is, of course, the frequency with which Watson is deceived. His old friend worries for his health in *The Reigate Squires* and, in a rare ebullient moment in the generally sombre *Final Problem*, Holmes assumes the last of many disguises and convinces Watson that he is condemned to travel with a doddery, non-English-speaking Italian priest.

**Narration**

## Narration

The narrative style of the Sherlock Holmes stories depends upon various factors, the main one of which is the use of Dr Watson as narrator. The note on Watson in **Who's who** suggests why he is such an admirable narrator, but he also has the advantage of being eyewitness of, or participant in, most of the events. However, he is not omniscient: the things that he is not told enable Holmes to astound us all by his feats of detection. Almost as important as Watson's narration is the use of narrative by the clients. Some stories consist of little more than two or three narratives, with Holmes' deductions and solution. There is a classic form to many (though by no means all) of the stories: visitor to Baker Street, feats of deduction from Holmes about him/her, long narrative appealing for Holmes' help, journey of detection, solution, followed by narrative explanation from Holmes. Thus the style and character of the client/narrators are crucial to the interest of the stories.

**Danger**

## Danger

The danger factor is very variable in these stories: several require little more than logical deduction and there is not the sense of ever-present danger associated with, for instance, American crime novels. There is the tension of imminent danger in stories like *The Greek Interpreter* and *The Five Orange Pips*; Holmes himself is alert for physical confrontation (as in *The Naval Treaty* and the frightening climax of *The Copper Beeches*) and suffers a murderous attack in *The Reigate Squires*. However, it is only in *The Final Problem* that we feel evil stalking the London streets and invading Baker Street and Watson's consulting-room.

## Essays/Examiner's tip icon

This icon is used to draw attention to a section of the **Text commentary** that is particularly relevant to either the section on **How to write a coursework essay** or to the section on **How to write an examination essay**. Each time it is used, a note identifies which section it relates to and adds a comment, quotation or piece of advice.

# The Adventures of Sherlock Holmes

## A Scandal in Bohemia

*The King of Bohemia, who is about to marry a princess, employs Holmes to obtain an incriminating photograph from his former mistress, the opera singer, beauty and adventuress, Irene Adler, who is now living in London. Whilst keeping her under observation, Holmes becomes involved as witness in her wedding to a lawyer, Godfrey Norton. An elaborate series of deceptions enables Holmes to locate the photograph at her house, Briony Lodge, but she proves his equal in observation, intuition and disguise. In turn she follows him to Baker Street in male clothing, then escapes him the following morning. A letter explains that the King has nothing to fear from blackmail.*

### The great detective

This is one of a number of stories where there is no crime (except by Holmes  and Watson) and a rarity in that Holmes fails. The ending reveals, in fact, that he was not needed anyway: Irene Adler has found a better man and will not betray the King. What is also unusual is his cheerful acceptance of Irene Adler's deception of him: his respect for a worthy opponent suggests that his interest is in the game, the puzzle, the testing of wits.

It is in this respect that Holmes emerges as 'the great detective' in this story. Re-read the three or so pages between the arrival of Dr Watson and the arrival of the King and see how many examples of ingenious logical deduction you can find.

Deduction

You will, however, notice a device that Conan Doyle often uses to reinforce the fame and abilities of Holmes: Watson's absence for some time serves as an excuse for a list of major international crimes that Holmes has solved (second paragraph of the story).

## The Woman

Irene Adler is presented as a unique person. She is, in a sense, Holmes' 'enemy' in the story, but he gains far more respect for her than for his rather pompous client. Make a list of the qualities that make Irene Adler so impressive: look at the effect she has on the 'horsey men' of Serpentine Mews as well as on Holmes, Watson and the King. Examine the qualities she shows in her earlier life, in London and in her final disappearance from the story. What feelings does Irene Adler inspire in Sherlock Holmes? Compare the first paragraph ('It was not that he felt any emotion akin to love ... ') with the final request for a photograph.

### Detective stories

The ambiguous nature of the relationship between detective and attractive female client/victim/criminal is to be found in many stories: a surprising number of fictional detectives are in no permanent relationship and many regret it, though not, apparently, Holmes.

## Disguise and adventure

Sherlock Holmes' powers of disguise are presented as being prodigious

Deception

throughout these stories, but this must be one of the most elaborate. Not only is he variously a groom and a clergyman, but he pretends to be seriously injured, employs a street-full of disguised extras (the King of Bohemia's generous expenses, no doubt), sees through the King's feeble disguise and is ultimately deceived (even as to her sex) by Irene Adler. This

spirit of adventure which works in parallel with the intellectual deductions, also shows itself in a splendid disregard for the law: 'You don't mind breaking the law?' he asks Watson and the respectable doctor replies, 'Not in the least.'

## Holmes' Boswell

Holmes describes Watson as 'my Boswell' because James Boswell wrote a

Dr Watson

famous *Life of Samuel Johnson* drawing on years of close acquaintance in which he recorded Dr Johnson's words and actions in detail. At the beginning of this story Watson has not seen Holmes for some time, but soon he assumes his usual role, the most important part of which is to emphasise Holmes' deductive and theatrical genius. As well as being a

most appreciative audience, he receives Holmes' damning judgement ('You see, but you do not observe'), yet is still sufficiently admiring to attempt Holmes' methods for himself.

## Society scandal

Conan Doyle's picture of European high society in the late nineteenth century is convincing, if pleasingly exaggerated. He amusingly creates a world of fabulously rich monarchs charmed by beautiful and talented 'adventuresses', a world where kings are their own diplomatic services and a scandal can bring down a monarchy. Note the splendidly pompous titles (both kingdoms are real places, though neither of them had a king in the nineteenth century) and the mixture of deference and scorn with which Holmes treats the King of Bohemia: re-read their final conversation.

# The Red-Headed League

*Jabez Wilson, a red-headed pawnbroker, comes to visit Holmes to complain of the sudden loss of his salary from the Red-Headed League. For eight weeks he was employed for four hours a day to copy out the Encyclopaedia Britannica at four pounds a week, until a notice announced the end of the Red-Headed League. Holmes, little interested in Wilson's complaint, believes that a serious crime is to be committed and his main interest centres on Wilson's new assistant who works for half-pay, drew his attention to the Red-Headed League and is looking after his business in his absence. An investigation of the area prompts Holmes to the belief that a raid is to be made on the City and Suburban Bank via a tunnel from Wilson's house. Holmes, Watson, Jones of Scotland Yard and Mr Merryweather of the Bank await the arrival of master-criminal John Clay (whom Holmes has recognised as the pawnbroker's assistant) and his accomplice. Arrests are made and Holmes explains his reasoning.*

### Mr Wilson's story

Jabez Wilson is a not an untypical figure in the Sherlock Holmes stories: the

*The victims*

perplexed, aggrieved figure telling a story in Baker Street, a story that does not appear to make sense, but which sets off a quite unexpected series of surmises from Sherlock Holmes. In this case he is frequently presented in a humorous way: the absurdity of his story and the fact that he is not in danger help the comic view of his character. At the end of his tale Holmes and Watson 'burst out into a roar of laughter'. What aspects of Wilson's character and narrative prompt this reaction?

Deduction

How do you react to Wilson's claim early in the story that 'I thought at first you had done something clever, but I see that there was nothing in it at all.'? To appreciate the humour, read Holmes' previous speech carefully.

## Narrative method

The formula used here is common to many Sherlock Holmes stories: the

Narration

victim's tale, interrupted by comments, questions and remarkable feats of deduction, takes nearly half of the story. The central section is mainly for Holmes to investigate the matter and meditate on the evidence. Holmes then sets up the final adventure (Watson's army revolver at the ready) and only after the arrest explains his reasoning.

Deception

The opening narrative is deliberately deceptive: people and places are not what they seem and the Red-Headed League, despite the title of the story, is not really the issue. The evidence is there, but it offers an oblique, sideways view of the case.

## John Clay, master-criminal

Note how the presentation of John Clay as a master-criminal reflects credit

The criminals

on Holmes. What evidence is there of his unique qualities? There is a certain boldly upper-class style about him (you will find the best examples at the time of his arrest) and his scheme was ingenious, but mainly the evidence comes in Holmes' comments. He recognises Clay instantly from Wilson's description, he recalls 'one or two little turns' with him and

he gives him such glowing testimonials as 'in my judgement, the fourth smartest man in London'. Think about what all this tells us about Holmes.

## Victorian London

Note the details of streets and journeys. Forms of transport (the hansom cab,

London

the new Underground system) are meticulously recorded and the age of the traffic jam is already here. A typical Conan Doyle sentence, atmospheric, yet factual, comes as the four men approach the bank: 'We rattled through an endless labyrinth of gas-lit streets until we emerged into Farringdon Street.'

---

**Detective stories**

It was Raymond Chandler, creator of the American private eye Philip Marlowe, who wrote memorably, 'Down these mean streets a man must go who is not himself mean.' The placing of the detective in his environment is crucial to the crime novel.

---

The police

Patrolling these cosmopolitan, murky, dangerous streets is a police force certain of its efficiency, yet marked by bungling incompetence. Conan Doyle set a trend by which the skills of the unofficial detective-hero are highlighted by police inefficiency. Inspector Lestrade is Conan Doyle's most unflattering police portrait: what qualities, good and bad, does Jones exhibit?

# A Case of Identity

*Mary Sutherland visits Holmes to ask him to find her missing fiancé, Hosmer Angel, who disappeared mysteriously when apparently on the way to their wedding. The story is an odd one, involving a young stepfather, Mr Windibank, who enjoys the income of Mary's legacy while she remains at home. The fact that he is always away from home (supposedly in France) when Hosmer meets her and various details (like a whispering voice) which suggest disguise in Hosmer lead Holmes to deduce that Hosmer does not exist. His demand that she pledge herself to be faithful to him was intended to secure Windibank's income. After gathering further evidence, Holmes unmasks the scoundrel who, sadly, cannot be prosecuted.*

## The puzzle

Here the emphasis on deductive powers at the expense of action is almost total.

Deduction

The tone is light: there is no hint of danger and Holmes clearly regards the whole thing as an engaging canter for his intellect. Even his fury at the scoundrel Windibank ends in laughter as he throws himself down in the chair from which he has conducted most of the investigation. The opening pages of the story invite speculation and deduction, with Watson serving as admiring straight man. After that the story is no more than two interviews: a long one with Miss Sutherland, a rather shorter one with her stepfather a day later, each followed by a summary of findings in conversation with Watson.

Deception

Conan Doyle presents many masters of disguise in these stories, not only Holmes himself. In this story the evidence is presented fairly to the reader. Make your own lists of evidence for Mr Windibank being Hosmer Angel. The first, based on the earlier interview, should include Windibank's motives, signs of disguise and other deceptions. The second, much shorter, should detail the confirmatory evidence Holmes obtains the next day.

## The professional crime-breaker?

Sherlock Holmes is a consulting detective: that is his profession. However, several of the cases give no indication of financial gain: how does the man make a living? It is very important that he remains outside the official channels.

---

**Contrast: procedurals**

The consulting or private detective is presented as an independent figure, pursuing the cases of interest (finance permitting). The case of Miss Mary Sutherland is typical: no doubt in a police story she would be no more than an irritation to the desk sergeant.

---

This little puzzle (not a crime, barely a story) suggests the two sides of Sherlock Holmes admirably. Watson describes him humorously as 'unofficial adviser and helper to everybody who is absolutely puzzled', but at the same time Holmes mentions some ten or twelve cases he is engaged on that are 'important ... without being interesting'. He also displays rich gifts from the ruling families of Bohemia and Holland. So why do we not see these cases? Sometimes, of course, as with *A Scandal in Bohemia*, we do but, according to Holmes, 'the larger crimes are apt to be the simpler'.

## Miss Mary Sutherland

Apart from the puzzle itself, the major interest in this story is Mary Sutherland,

an attractive study in credulity, warm–heartedness, affection, devotion, just a little stupidity and the first beginnings of a sense of independence that we hope will prove painful to Windibank in the future. Note the detailed description of her appearance: what do you think it suggests about her character and situation? Also consider in what ways Mary Sutherland can be described as a 'victim': of whom or what is she a victim?

# The Boscombe Valley Mystery

*Sherlock Holmes summons Watson to help him with a problem in Herefordshire. Charles McCarthy, a local farmer who formerly lived in Australia, has been beaten to death near Boscombe Pool. The obvious suspect, already arrested, is his son James who quarrelled with him immediately before the murder. McCarthy senior was determined that his son should marry the daughter of the local landowner, John Turner, whose fortune had been made in Australia. Despite Inspector Lestrade's certainty of young McCarthy's guilt, Holmes' investigations reveal a quite different story: James loves Alice Turner, but is already married (mercifully his wife now reveals the existence of an earlier husband!); Turner has been blackmailed by the older McCarthy for crimes in Australia; Turner is now dying and admits killing McCarthy in a letter to be used if James is found guilty, but hopes to die a free man; he has this wish when James is found not guilty.*

## 'Someone... on whom I can thoroughly rely'

Holmes seeks out Watson to help him: though his presence and participation

*Dr Watson*

are always welcome to Holmes, it is less often that Holmes expressly states a need for him. Try to work out what Watson contributes to Holmes' investigation. One regular feature of Watson's role is to be a foil to Holmes' brilliance, and you will find an excellent example of this when Watson examines the verbatim account of the trial. Later, shortly before the appearance of John Turner, Holmes says, 'I don't quite know what to do, and I should value your advice.' This is a remarkable statement for Holmes to make: what exactly does he want Watson to advise him on?

*The police*

Watson is, of course, a sensible antidote to Inspector Lestrade, treated by Holmes with the utmost contempt. Look at the description of the inspector when they first arrive in Ross and examine Holmes' various conversations with him (about such things as the botching of evidence at the pool) until Holmes finally gives up on any chance of making him understand: 'I have given you the chance. Here are your lodgings. Good-bye.'

## Man of intellect, man of action

In Holmes Conan Doyle wished to create an intellectual superman, but also

*Sherlock Holmes*

an eccentric of unexpected talents and weaknesses. Notice the bizarre opening conversation with Lestrade: he does not wish to visit the scene of the crime while the barometric pressure is high (why does he say this?) and he has 'a caseful of cigarettes ... which need smoking'. The suggestion of humour is obvious, but the most interesting feature of Holmes' conduct is the contrast of intellect and action. On the journey to Ross, he prefers his pocket edition of Petrarch (a fourteenth-century Italian poet) to the case and later insists on talking about the poet and novelist George Meredith and leaving the investigation to the next day. Compare this to the passage beginning 'Sherlock Holmes was transformed...' when he investigates the scene of the crime.

## A complicated narrative

*The Boscombe Valley Mystery* has a more complicated narrative pattern than many of the Sherlock Holmes stories: it does not depend simply on retrieving incriminating documents or seeing through a disguise. There is a lengthy series of relationships, deceptions and 'red herrings' to understand: what appears to be Turner's generosity (a sign of friendship) is in fact the result of McCarthy's blackmail (the exact opposite), young McCarthy's motives for refusing Miss Turner are concealed, etc. For once the narrator who sets up the story is Holmes himself, presenting the complications with clarity.

Narration

Another element of interest in the narration is that, though Sherlock Holmes solves the case, his findings as told by Watson do not affect the court case. Instead 'a number of objections which had been drawn out by Holmes' (no details given) win the case for James McCarthy.

## Criminals and victims

The criminals

You might like to consider Holmes' attitude to justice and the law: is it reasonable to keep the murderer's identity secret? Who are the villains in this story and who are the victims? Sherlock Holmes' confidence in his own justice and morality would, of course, be incompatible with the duty of a law enforcement officer.

The victims

You should have no difficulty in perceiving where Conan Doyle places Holmes' and the reader's sympathy. Miss Turner has claims as his employer, but even more as a typically idealised example of devoted Victorian womanhood.

# The Five Orange Pips

*John Openshaw visits Holmes with the account of the mysterious deaths of his uncle and father, both apparently accidental, shortly after each received a request for papers in the name of 'K.K.K.', plus five orange pips, in the mail. The uncle, though based in Sussex at the time of his death, had been a planter in Florida and left the United States in the aftermath of the Civil War: reputedly he suffered from 'aversion to the negroes'. Holmes advises Openshaw to leave a single remaining sheet relating to his American days (his uncle having burned the rest) on the sundial as requested, whilst he investigates. Openshaw has, however, waited too long to seek Holmes' advice and is drowned near Waterloo Bridge. Holmes discovers who the Ku Klux Klan members are — the captain and mates of the* Lone Star *sailing out of Georgia - but his revenge is prevented when the ship is lost with all hands.*

## Mystery and menace

This is really a story of a different type from the normal detective story. In Victorian times British readers enjoyed reading rather melodramatic tales of curses and mysterious revenges from exotic corners of the world. With India under British rule, colonies in Australasia, Africa and the Americas, and trade opening up into China, Japan and the rest of the Orient, it was easy to believe that a delinquent past would bring terror into the lives of apparently respectable citizens of London or the Home Counties. Conan Doyle enterprisingly chooses the setting of the USA for the evil deeds. Holmes takes a fairly passive role in the story. It is interesting that even he has to look up the Ku Klux Klan: though originally founded at the end of the Civil War, the Klan in its modern form is a twentieth-century creation.

Narration

The narrative method stresses horror rather than the astounding deductive skills of Holmes, though there is the customary display when the client arrives. In the first paragraph Watson, looking back on the case, describes it as 'remarkable' and 'startling' and, surprisingly for a detective story, tells us that there are points which 'never have been ... entirely cleared up.' Though the main story emerges, these, in fact, are quite crucial points: you should be able to think of at least three.

Danger

Everything exudes menace and mystery. Examine the reaction of Openshaw's uncle on the arrival of the letter from Pondicherry: his physical appearance and tone of voice as well as the words he says. Or re-read the third paragraph for Watson's description of the weather before John Openshaw's arrival.

Rather than admiring the great detective's ingenuity, the reader is expected to chill with horror: even Holmes raves and waves clenched fists at the police neglect of the danger and is moved to a revenge which the seas render unnecessary.

# The Man with the Twisted Lip

*Dr Watson visits an opium den late at night in a successful attempt to restore an addicted family friend to his wife. He is accosted by a heavily disguised Sherlock Holmes. The case which Holmes is investigating involves the disappearance and possible murder of*

*Neville St. Clair, a city businessman living in Kent. The previous Monday Mrs St. Clair, on an unexpected trip to London, saw her husband reacting frantically, then disappearing, from a second floor window above the opium den. All the evidence (blood, clothes, a present for his son) points to St. Clair having been there and having been murdered by Hugh Boone, a crippled and disfigured beggar who lodges in the room. Then Mrs St. Clair receives a letter saying that her husband is safe. A sleepless night spent consuming an ounce of shag tobacco brings the solution to Holmes and, with the aid of a sponge, he reveals Boone as St. Clair whose 'respectable' city job was begging in Threadneedle Street!*

## Appearance and reality

The disguise assumed by Neville St. Clair is such that 'even a wife's eyes could not pierce so complete a disguise'. That assumed by Sherlock Holmes is, of course, equally effective: his oldest friend sees him as merely 'a tall, thin old man' and 'very wrinkled, bent with age'. Holmes we must accept as a master of disguise: what reason is given for St. Clair's skill?

There is also deception in the narration of this story. The opening sentence, filled with dignity, suggests that Isa Whitney is to be the subject of the story; his wife's arrival, grief-stricken, late at night, seeking assistance, is almost a parody of a typical opening, except that the visitor comes to Watson's house, not 221B, Baker Street. However, Whitney is simply a pretext for the meeting of Holmes and Watson in Upper Swandam Lane.

### Examiner's tip
This is a fine example of the change of narrative method. 'Oh! I'm in such trouble! I do so want a little help.' cries Kate Whitney, having arrived distraught late at night, but the appeal is to the Watsons, not Holmes, and she is not the subject of the story.

Kate Whitney, the devoted, concerned wife is, however, a typical Conan Doyle victim: compare her to Mrs St. Clair and try to remember similar characters in other stories.

*The victims*

## Capital of Empire

The picture of London in the Sherlock Holmes stories may strike us as quaint and comfortable in some ways, but Conan Doyle also presents the violent and disreputable side of the capital of Empire very vividly. Upper Swandam Lane lies behind river wharves that line the Port of London; the opium den is run by a 'rascally Lascar' (Indian seaman) and 'sallow' Malays; it even resembles 'the forecastle of an emigrant ship'.

**London**

**Danger**

There is no crime committed as part of the story, though there are criminals around: why else should the Lascar have 'sworn vengeance upon' Holmes? Despite the use of criminal and racial stereotypes, Conan Doyle is at pains to reveal the shallowness of respectability. Isa Whitney's brother is principal of a theological college, but Isa ruins himself by helpless addiction. Neville St. Clair, ex-reporter with a highly respectable background, disguises himself to beg. Note, too, that his reasons for this are financial: society does not reward honest toil so well as deception.

# ■ Self-test questions – *A Scandal in Bohemia* to *The Man with the Twisted Lip*

### Who? What? When? Where? How? Why?
1    Who is 'obese, pompous and low', with 'blazing red hair'?
2    Who received a letter from Pondicherry?
3    Who lives at Briony Lodge?
4    Who sits on a three-legged stool by 'a small brazier of burning charcoal'?
5    What did Ezekiah Hopkins (reputedly) find?
6    What is the true meaning of 'a rat' in the McCarthy murder?
7    What is Mr Windibank's occupation?
8    Where did McCarthy and Turner first meet?
9    When does 'sitting upon five cushions and consuming an ounce of shag' solve a mystery?
10   Where is the ship *Lone Star* based?
11   Where is John Clay arrested?
12   How does 'Hosmer Angel' go missing on the way to his wedding?
13   How do the Watsons help Kate Whitney?
14   Why did Colonel Elias Openshaw leave the United States?
15   Why did James McCarthy for so long refuse to marry Miss Turner?

### Important clues
What is the significance of the following clues, either in solving crimes or in demonstrating Holmes' expertise?
1    'Six almost parallel cuts' in Watson's left shoe
2    The keenness on photography of Jabez Wilson's assistant
3    A box of bricks
4    A cry of 'Cooee!'
5    Letters from Pondicherry, Dundee and London
6    Footprints by Boscombe Pool
7    'A hesitating, whispering fashion of speech'
8    A double line on the plush sleeve of a dress
9    A watermark of 'Eg P Gt'
10   £220 credit in the Capital and Counties Bank

### Who said this about what or whom?
1    'Now I wonder who the deuce that could have been.'

2   'The case is as plain as a pikestaff, and the more one goes into it the plainer it becomes.'
3   'Oh, a trusty comrade is always of use. And a chronicler still more so.'
4   'We have known each other since we were little children, and I know his faults as no one else does, but he is too tender-hearted to hurt a fly.'
5   'My God, my God, my sins have overtaken me.'

**Follow the theme**
1   What evidence is there in these six stories of Holmes' attitude to the law and the police?
2   Examine the six cases brought before Holmes and work out:
    a)  which ones relate to a crime;
    b)  in which ones the complainant is aware what the offence is;
    c)  in which a criminal is brought to justice.

# The Blue Carbuncle

*Peterson, the Baker Street commissionaire, has acquired a Christmas goose in the aftermath of a street fight. Peterson's wife discovers in the bird's crop the Countess of Morcar's blue carbuncle, incredibly valuable and recently stolen. A plumber, John Horner, is to stand trial for its theft in the Hotel Cosmopolitan on the evidence of James Ryder, upper-attendant at the hotel. Having found the owner of the goose, Henry Baker, Holmes follows the trail of innocent men from him to the landlord of the Alpha Inn to Breckenridge the salesman. The trail is about to lead to Mrs Oakshott of Brixton Road when the timely arrival of James Ryder simplifies matters. Finally the truth is told: he and the countess' maid arranged the theft and framed Horner, but then, searching for a hiding place, forced the stone down the throat of one of Mrs Oakshott's birds, only to take the wrong bird and leave the rest to be delivered to Breckenridge. Holmes allows the pathetic Ryder to leave, convinced that Horner is safe from conviction now that Ryder is silenced.*

## Sherlock Holmes: law enforcer?

Deduction

This story is an excellent example of Holmes' distance from the law and the police. He feels no compulsion to bring wrong-doers to court: his delight is the deductive process, not the comparatively harmless criminal captured.

The opening six or so pages are well worth studying as a good example of Holmes' method. No precious stone having yet been found in the goose, the whole affair merely provides him with the amusement of logical speculation. This he carries out with due earnestness, examining the hat that belongs to the owner of the goose with lens and forceps. Examine the conclusions he reaches from the study of the hat: do you find them impressive, convincing, far-fetched? Certainly you will not be able to fault the powers of observation and logic.

The criminals

You might also find Holmes' reaction to discovering the criminal surprising. The countess's jewel is returned, Horner will not be found guilty, so Holmes cannot bring himself to take action against the snivelling wretch who is guilty. Is he just not interested or does he have some other motive? Read the last paragraph for a surprisingly modern (or simply Christian?) view of rehabilitation.

## A Merry Christmas

This is one of the most humorous of the Sherlock Holmes stories, beginning with something of a parody of Holmes at work, investigating a battered hat with lens and forceps. The narrative of John Ryder offers the irresistible image of his forcing the stone down the bird's throat, then, having persuaded his sister to give him that particular goose, finding that there is another identical bird. Holmes himself is in jovial mood and his last words are of the delights of the Christmas table.

Much of the humour comes from the dialogue with assorted Cockney characters: Baker, whose intellectual circle meets at the Alpha Inn (after study

### Examiner's tip

The place of humour in giving variety to the Sherlock Holmes stories should not be under-estimated. There are frequently hints of dry humour in Holmes himself. Here we have some farcical moments, comical characters, and Holmes clearly amusing himself.

in the Museum, of course), the landlord, Breckenridge who is understandably annoyed at the attention the goose is getting, but who cannot resist a bet and tells Holmes all.

London

Even Mrs Oakshott, calmly telling her brother she could never tell the barred-tailed birds apart, emerges as a real character.

# The Speckled Band

*Helen Stoner arrives at Holmes' rooms in a state of terror. She is the step-daughter of Dr Grimesby Roylott, a violent man who spent years in India and now associates only with gipsies, and has such exotic pets as a baboon and a cheetah. Helen's mother is now dead, and two years previously her sister died in mysterious circumstances: a strange whistling disturbed her sleep for some nights, and on the night of her death she appeared transfixed, able only to shriek, 'The speckled band!'. She had been about to marry and now Helen is planning to do the same; her step-father has moved her to her sister's bedroom next to his and the whistling has recurred. Despite a warning from the maniacal Dr Roylott, Holmes and Watson head for Stoke Moran, examine the house and wait the night in Helen's bedroom. Holmes' deduction proves correct: Dr Roylott sends a swamp adder (the speckled band) through a ventilator to kill Helen, Holmes' cane drives it back and the murderer is poisoned.*

## A classic detective story

Of all the stories in *The Adventures of Sherlock Holmes*, *The Speckled Band* is probably the one that most successfully combines all the qualities of a classic detective story. Interestingly enough, Conan Doyle has seen fit to revive the classic domestic arrangement: Watson recalls the story as happening some years previously when he and Holmes shared the Baker Street rooms, and Mrs Hudson the landlady reappears.

Thus Watson is there as Holmes' 'intimate friend and associate' when the story begins at 7.15 in the morning. The character of Helen Stoner sets the tone for the story: shivering with fear, 'her face all drawn and grey, with restless frightened eyes, like those of some hunted animal.' She is obviously a sensible and level-headed woman; therefore there must be a good reason for her terror.

## Terror at Stoke Moran

Stoke Moran offers a range of terrors. The mystery of her sister's death, in circumstances she is now repeating, terrifies Helen, but there is far more to fear at Stoke Moran. All the descriptions of Dr Roylott inspire fear, and his brief appearance at Baker Street suggests an elemental force of evil. Re-read the descriptive paragraph when he first appears in the doorway and note the adjectives and comparisons applied to him.

Then there are the dangers of the exotic East, the baboon and the cheetah, blameless, as it turns out. Equally blameless are the gipsies, but they add an air of menace as well as providing the 'red herring' of 'the speckled band'. The house itself is crumbling: the description as Holmes and Watson approach suggests the eerie atmosphere of an ancient haunted manor. As it happens, the danger comes from recent changes to the most modern part of the house, but the terror of Helen Stoner, living in such a house with a violent and abusive step-father, is readily to be understood.

## The mystery

Central to any detective story, however, is the detection. *The Speckled Band* is one of the finest Sherlock Holmes stories, with its mix of suggestive clues, intellectual deduction, exposure to danger and appropriate ending.

Danger

The mystery is far more than a mere puzzle. Holmes and Watson sit through four hours of darkness, weapons at the ready, judging events merely by the sounds emanating from Dr Roylott's room, a brief flurry of action moves Holmes to 'horror and loathing', a 'dreadful shriek' strikes cold to their hearts and the villain is dead.

The reader is given most of the clues for what is a classic 'locked room' mystery.

Deduction

---

**Detective stories**

The 'whodunnit' element is, of course, important in the detective story and this is a very satisfying story from that point of view: more 'How was it done?', maybe. But this classic detective story has much more: the dramatic setting, the terrifying Roylott, Holmes' and Watson's vigil in the dark, etc.

---

We know Dr Roylott wishes Helen dead for financial reasons, we know he is vicious and unhinged and has moved her room to murder her, but how will he succeed when her room is locked and bolted and does not communicate with his? Examine Miss Stoner's narration and, especially, the account of Holmes' examination of the two bedrooms, and make a list of clues, noting what is unusual in each case and how it fits into the murder plot. You could start with:

New bell-pull        Not attached to bell        A 'bridge' for snake to use

# The Engineer's Thumb

*Early one morning Victor Hatherley, a hydraulic engineer, comes to Dr Watson with his thumb hacked off and a strange tale to tell. Watson takes him to Holmes and the tale unfolds. He was visited the previous evening by a German, calling himself Colonel Lysander Stark, for the purpose of repairing a stamping machine. The purpose of the machine (compressing fuller's earth) sounds highly unlikely and the fact that this is to be done in the middle of the night is suspicious, but the fee is tempting. The engineer takes a train to Eyford, is then taken by carriage to the house and diagnoses the fault. When he reveals his suspicions, Stark attempts to grind the engineer to death in the machine.*

*His escape is made at the expense of his thumb, chopped off by Stark/Fritz's cleaver. A visit to the site by Holmes and the police reveals that the house has burnt down (thanks to the engineer's lantern) and the coiners (for that is what they are) have escaped.*

## A nocturnal adventure

Holmes contributes very little to this story. It is little more than four pages before the end of the story that Hatherley's narration finishes. Holmes has asked some pertinent questions about the horse and carriage that later enable him to find the site of the house: very close to the station. As the story finishes, he confirms one element in it by means of his filing system. A mysterious German woman twice tried to save Hatherley, the second time saying to Fritz: 'Remember your promise after the last time.' Holmes finds a cutting which tells of an engineer's mysterious disappearance a year previously.

Holmes' last words sum up the story. More a mysterious adventure than a detective story, it will give the engineer the chance to dine out on it for the rest of his life: he will 'gain the reputation of being excellent company'. This is very much the victim's story; the villains remain shrouded in mystery. Who is that good-hearted Elise: eager, beautiful and sick with fear? How did she become involved with the psychopathically cruel Fritz? What part does the well-fed 'Ferguson' (who apparently has a conscience) play in the whole enterprise?

The victims

# The Noble Bachelor

*Lord St. Simon contacts Sherlock Holmes with a view to solving the mystery of the disappearance of his bride, Hatty Doran, during the wedding breakfast. She is an American whose father has only recently become rich after years of mining for gold. The suspicion of Inspector Lestrade falls on Flora Miller, a dancer 'devotedly attached' to Lord Doran, and his views are confirmed by finding Hatty's clothes in the Serpentine with a note in the pocket signed 'F.H.M.'. However, Holmes has always been convinced that she has simply returned to a former lover or existing husband and these initials, plus the hotel bill the note is written on, lead him to Mr and Mrs Francis Hay Moulton, re-united after a long series of misadventures and misunderstandings. Lord St. Simon accepts the situation, though hardly graciously.*

## A romance

The method of narration is unusual and effective, consisting of a series of narratives or dialogues presenting different viewpoints on the same events. So far as the reader is concerned, everything comes to Baker Street: we hear and see the results of Lestrade's splashing around in the Serpentine or Holmes' visits to hotels and the Moulton residence rather than

Narration

following them on their investigations. Compare the views of the case of the different narratives: Watson's readings from the newspapers, Lord St. Simon's account prompted by Holmes, Lestrade's presentation of evidence to Holmes' mocking scrutiny, and the Moultons' story as told at supper. The story itself is a romance, perhaps rather far-fetched, but containing many of the elements of romance, notably the poor boy made good, the secret marriage and the hero missing, presumed dead (captured by the Apaches, no less!).

## Holmes and authority

The police (the unfortunate Lestrade) are again presented with an element of

The police

mockery, both by the author and by his chief character. Note Holmes' 'innocent' questions and ironic compliments as the inspector, shrieking and tapping his head, becomes increasingly confused by the detective's actions. Is Lestrade as stupid as he is made to appear? The coincidence of initials is unfortunate for him, though you might also conclude that Holmes' awareness of the bouquet trick and question about whether the bride could see the street are simple common-sense that should not have been beyond a police inspector.

The aristocratic Lord St. Simon is treated with no more deference than the

Sherlock Holmes

police, if with somewhat more politeness. The opening suggests that nothing dreadful is going to happen and the story always has something of a humorous tinge. Consider the use of ironic humour in the title. In the story itself Lord St. Simon's rather absurd obsession with family is amusingly deflated by Holmes' 'No, I am descending' soon after his entry.

# The Beryl Coronet

*The banker Alexander Holder comes to Baker Street so distraught that he appears mad. The previous day he advanced £50,000 to an eminent lord who gave as security the Beryl Coronet. Terrified of theft, Holder took it home. He has a son, Arthur, whom he regards as disreputable (he is associated with the dangerous Sir George Burnwell) and an adoptive daughter Mary, apparently saintly and the subject of Arthur's devotion. In the middle of the night Holder was awoken by a sound to see Arthur wrenching at the coronet from which a corner with three beryls has been ripped. He is convinced of Arthur's guilt; Holmes is convinced of his innocence. Holmes' investigations centre around footprints in the snow, and by the following morning he has the missing jewels for Holder who by now is stricken by Mary's leaving home. Sir George is the common factor: he had an 'understanding' with Mary and persuaded her to steal the coronet (rescued, damaged, by Arthur); he sells the jewels (which Holmes buys) and flees with Mary.*

## Heroes and villains

The opening of *The Beryl Coronet* is one of the most striking of introductions

of one of Holmes' clients, with Watson's words, 'Holmes, here is a madman coming along', followed by a remarkably graphic description of a dignified man giving his legs unaccustomed exercise in his despairing haste. Alexander Holder proves a well-drawn and three-dimensional character with clearly defined moral and professional standards, a convincing mixture of worldliness and innocence. He also provides an effective contrast to Holmes' methods of reasoning. To him it is perfectly clear that his son is guilty: he was caught red-handed. Read Sherlock Holmes' summary of Holder's views in the paragraph beginning ' "Now, my dear sir," said Holmes…' just before they depart for Streatham. As a scenario it is patently absurd: why then does the intelligent Mr Holder believe it?

Heroes and villains cannot be taken at face value. Throughout the Holmes stories people are not who they seem to be: in this case the difficulty is not who they are, but what sort of people they are. Mary appears to be the sort of character that Conan Doyle idealises in other stories: a young woman of intelligence and strength of character, but devoted and unselfish in her emotions. How far is that description accurate in her case?

## The way to the truth

In place of preconceptions and assumptions Holmes offers deduction from given facts, with imaginative inferences which then can be checked against evidence (as in the link to Sir George).

Deduction

---

**Detective stories**

The preconceptions of others are part of the fabric of most detective stories. When all seems obvious, Holmes and his successors disagree: 'A likely story!', says Holmes. 'As if a man bent on felony would slam the door so as to awake a household.'

---

His detailed account of what he learned from the snow around the house (last 3–4 pages) is a fine demonstration of Holmes' method, though we might think the maid's sweetheart with the wooden leg was something of a gift to the great detective! Above all, this section contains the classic definition of

Holmes' art: 'It is an old maxim of mine that when you have excluded the impossible, whatever remains, however improbable, must be the truth.'

# The Copper Beeches

*Violet Hunter, a governess, consults Holmes about a strange situation she has been offered: she is to receive a remarkably high salary for looking after Jephro Rucastle's young son at the Copper Beeches near Winchester, on condition that she wears a certain dress, sits in a certain place and has her long hair cut off. Eventually she accepts, but two weeks later summons Holmes and Watson to Winchester. The situation is becoming intolerable. She has noticed a young man looking from the road when she has had to sit facing away from the window wearing a dress belonging to Alice, Rucastle's daughter by his first marriage. The inhabitants include a drunken groom, Toller, and a mastiff only he can control. She finds an identical coil of hair to her own in a chest of drawers and a secret suite of rooms, one with locked door and shuttered windows. Holmes deduces that Alice is imprisoned there and plans to rescue her that night. As it turns out, Fowler, her lover, has bribed Mrs Toller to assist and has already eloped with her. In the resulting confusion, the dog savages Rucastle, and Holmes and Watson slip away.*

## What danger?

Things are seldom what they seem in Holmes stories. A terrible crime may

Danger

prove to be nothing at all; disappearing people may never have existed. Here a tamely domestic problem leads to a violent melodrama with locked rooms, cruel jailers and a giant dog patrolling the grounds. However, this is placed in a typically English setting. Not only the situation of the Copper Beeches, but also much of the motivation and behaviour of Mr Rucastle, place this firmly in middle-class Victorian England, not the ruined castles and mad counts of a 'Gothic' romance.

Examine Rucastle's motives for his treatment of Alice: dislike between step-mother and daughter is only a small part of it. Read Mrs Toller's account at the end of the story and you will come across a very middle-class materialistic motive for cruelty: in which other Holmes stories do you find a similar motive?

## A course of lectures or a series of tales?

Dr Watson

The opening of this story offers some indication as to why Holmes and Watson are seen by so many people almost as real historical characters. Not only is Watson a participant in the stories and their narrator, a common enough literary device, but here he discusses with the central character how effective the stories are. Holmes approves of the emphasis placed on apparently trivial stories rather than *causes célèbres* (famous cases) and disapproves of the emphasis on colour and personality at the expense of logic. Finally, we have the surreal situation of two characters in a fictional story arguing over whether the stories they appear in are too sensational! At this point Holmes, complaining of the decline in original crime, hands over a letter to prove he has been reduced to 'giving advice to young ladies from boarding schools'. This letter, of course, heralds a bizarre and dangerous adventure.

 Holmes has little influence on the main story-line of *The Copper Beeches* except to increase the possibilities of violence and crime. His reassurance prompts Violet Hunter to take the post and be brave enough to stay. The failure of Miss Hunter (and, at a distance, Holmes) to identify the key role of Mrs Toller brings a second escape attempt in one night and causes Mr Rucastle's mauling by the mastiff. No doubt Holmes would consider that deserved, but his decision to depart speedily is well-judged.

*The Copper Beeches* is a good example of a tale rather than a lecture and, of course, Holmes' claim that 'a course of lectures' would be preferable is groundless. The mystery is solved by action, more than logic, though Holmes' distant unravelling of the situation is impressive.

---

 **Contrast: procedurals**

*The Copper Beeches* is a good example of the concentration on one case permitted by the traditional detective story. 'At any time, day or night, a telegram would bring me down to your help.' Watson even anticipates the stirring of warmer feelings.

---

Holmes sees it purely as a case, with no claim on his emotions. During the story he may admire the charming and courageous Miss Hunter ('a quite exceptional woman'), but to the disappointment of the sentimental Dr Watson, he afterwards manifests 'no further interest in her' and she ends up teaching in Walsall!

# ■ Self-test questions – *The Blue Carbuncle* to *The Copper Beeches*

**Who? What? When? Where? How? Why?**

1  Who claims to be called John Robinson?
2  Whose accomplishments include 'a little French, a little German, music and drawing'?
3  Who has a wooden leg?
4  Who recommended Sherlock Holmes to Lord St. Simon?
5  What does 'Colonel Lysander Stark' claim to be doing near Eyford?
6  What is 'the speckled band'?

7   When does the story of *The Blue Carbuncle* begin?
8   When did Helen Stonor's sister, Julia, die?
9   Where did Aloysius Doran make his fortune?
10  Where does Holmes find the stones from the Beryl Coronet?
11  How does Alice Rucastle escape?
12  How does Lestrade confuse Lord St. Simon's former love with Hatty's husband?
13  How does Dr Roylott die?
14  Why does Rucastle wish to prevent Alice's marriage?
15  Why does Holmes let James Ryder escape?

## Important clues
What is the significance of the following clues, either in solving crimes or in demonstrating Holmes' expertise?
1   A bill from a hotel
2   Sir George Burnwell's shoe
3   A ventilator between two internal rooms
4   The smell of a cigar
5   A hat-securer with broken elastic
6   A double line of booted footprints and a double line of naked footprints
7   A bouquet dropped in church
8   A single horse pulling a carriage, fresh, not at all tired
9   A whistle and a metallic sound
10  A bed fixed to the floor

## Who said this about what or whom?
1   'The Scotland Yard jack-in-office'
2   'It is very good of… to honour my head by putting it on a level with his own.'
3   'But I'll have a sovereign on with you, just to teach you not to be obstinate.'
4   'The walls were of wood, but the floor consisted of a large iron trough, and when I went to examine it I could see a crust of metallic deposit all over it.'
5   'Crime is common. Logic is rare. Therefore it is upon the logic rather than the crime that you should dwell.'

## Follow the theme
1   Relationships between fathers and sons or daughters frequently play a significant part in these stories. Compare them and try to pick out any recurring themes.
2   What part is played in these stories by:
    a)   characters assuming other identities;
    b)   the location of the crimes?

# The Memoirs of Sherlock Holmes

## Silver Blaze

*The favourite for the Wessex Cup, Silver Blaze, has disappeared and his trainer John Straker been murdered. Holmes and Watson go to the stables on Dartmoor some days after the crime to find that Inspector Gregory has been unusually diligent. The obvious suspect is Fitzroy Simpson, a book-maker who stands to lose heavily on Silver Blaze. He appeared at the stables the night of the crime and offered money to the stable-lad who was guarding the horse and who was found drugged in the morning. There is, however, no solid evidence against him. Finding the horse proves to be straightforward: Holmes believes it would have gone to the neighbouring stables of Capleton, tracks lead that way and the horse is discovered disguised. Holmes returns to London having arranged a dramatic re-appearance for Silver Blaze at the Wessex Cup: the horse, of course, wins. Meanwhile an accumulation of pieces of evidence points to Straker as the one who removed the horse from King's Pyland stable. The story finally becomes clear: Straker planned to lame his own horse for a betting coup, but was struck down by Silver Blaze who then bolted towards Capleton.*

### The power of imagination

Sherlock Holmes is unusually favourable in his opinion of Inspector Gregory,

The police

who has gathered the evidence soundly, answers Holmes' questions authoritatively, puts forward sensible theories and 'surpasses himself' by providing boots and shoes to compare with the prints that he has carefully protected with matting. Compare his approach to the scene of the crime with Lestrade's in *The Boscombe Valley Mystery*. No wonder Holmes exclaims 'Excellent', as he also does to Watson who emerges at his most astute here, but this praise serves to reveal the unique deductive qualities of Holmes.

Deduction

Logic is always the key to Holmes' investigations, but here the importance of imagination is stressed. Holmes says of Gregory, 'Were he but gifted with imagination, he might rise to great heights in his profession'. You can find many examples of Holmes' imagination in the investigation, suggesting a line of action which he can then confirm by observation or questioning. Examine the role of imagination in the following instances:

- Madame Lesurier's milliner's bill made out to William Darbyshire;
- the choice of curry for the evening meal;
- the wax vesta (match) in the mud;
- the hoofprints leading to Capleton;
- the lame sheep.

In addition, there is perhaps the most famous example of Holmes' mix of imagination and logic in 'the curious incident of the dog in the night-time'. Only Holmes can grasp the importance of something not happening: the dog would have barked at a stranger.

### Detective stories

The uncomprehending audience is a regular feature of detective stories. Watson is sometimes called upon to play the role, but here an eager young detective engages in perplexed dialogue with Holmes: 'The dog did nothing in the night-time.'/'That was the curious incident.'

## Who is guilty?

Surprisingly often no one is arrested at the end of a Sherlock Holmes story.

This story is full of people just the right (or wrong) side of the law. The vicious crime turns out not to be a crime at all and the stealing of the horse almost unintentional. Silas Brown's crime is petty enough for Holmes to grant an amnesty; Fitzroy Simpson is up to no good, but does no harm; not for the first time in Holmes stories, a group of gipsies provide the 'red herring'; even John Straker's sins (betraying his wife, extravagance, an attempt to nobble his own horse) are trivial compared to his punishment.

# The Yellow Face

*Grant Munro tells of strange changes in his wife's behaviour and a mysterious arrival at the cottage near their home in Norbury. Munro married Effie Hebron, a young widow from Atlanta, Georgia, three years previously; her husband and child were dead. Their happy and trusting relationship has been recently disturbed by an unexplained request from her for a hundred pounds, the sight of a livid yellow face at the upstairs window of the cottage and inexplicable visits (the first in the middle of the night) by Effie to the cottage. Holmes is certain blackmail is afoot (perhaps her first husband is not dead, but mad or diseased, and she has fled to escape), but, when they break into the cottage, the answer proves to be a little black girl, daughter of Effie and her late husband, wearing a mask. The Grant Munros are reconciled and little Lucy finds a new home.*

## Even Holmes can be wrong

Narration

The narrative structure is based around the fact that this is one of Holmes' few errors. Watson's introduction stresses it and the last sentence reminds us of it, striking a rare note of wry humility from Holmes. A typical opening (distraught client tells his story at Baker Street) is delayed by the amusing episode of the walk in the park (Holmes indignantly blaming taking exercise for missing a client) and the customary display of expertise based on Grant Munro's pipe. The client's narrative is by far the longest part of the story, followed by Holmes' imaginative deductions, for once given in full before there is the evidence to prove them. Why does Conan Doyle include Holmes' lengthy exposition of the probability of blackmail?

## A domestic problem

The story is really of a domestic problem, of trust broken, then forged again on more open terms: 'I am not a very good man, Effie, but I think that I am a better one than you have given me credit for being' is the start of a new relationship and the message of the story. It is difficult now to accept the need to cover a black girl's face with a yellow mask, and you may find this story somewhat distasteful. However, though it may suggest shocking prejudice in Victorian England, as well as in Georgia, Conan Doyle clearly does not approve of such prejudice.

# The Stockbroker's Clerk

*Having just obtained a post at Mawson and Williams', Hall Pycroft is offered a large salary by 'Arthur Pinner', to serve as business manager of a new company in Birmingham. Two odd stipulations are made: he must write a letter accepting the post and he is not to tell Mawson's. In Birmingham the office is hardly occupied and he is given meaningless tasks to perform: eventually he recognises 'Arthur Pinner' and his brother in Birmingham as the same person. Holmes and Watson accompany Pycroft to Birmingham and meet 'Harry Pinner', who then disappears into an inner office and attempts to hang himself. As he recovers, Holmes explains the plot: having obtained a sample of Pycroft's handwriting, Pinner's accomplice has taken up Pycroft's post at Mawson's for criminal purposes. A newspaper article reveals the reason for the attempted suicide: an attempted robbery at Mawson and Williams' has resulted in the murder of a watchman and the arrest of the criminal, Beddington, whose brother is now sought as an accomplice. Holmes has, of course, found him.*

## The chirpy cockney

Hall Pycroft is an energetic and even cheerful person for the victim of a crime; indeed it is difficult to see him as a victim at all.

Many of the victims in the Holmes stories are characterised by innocence  and/or fear. Pycroft is 'a smart young City man' whose untypical look of grief is almost comical. Though much of the story is set in Birmingham, he is a typical Londoner, which gives his narrative a distinctive tone. Note his use of slang: in the first two paragraphs of his narration he has 'lost his crib' (job), has been 'a soft Johnny', 'come a nasty cropper', got 'a ripping good testimonial', found it 'a perfect frost' (nothing doing) and failed

London

to get a 'billet' (post). See what other examples you can find: there are even a few more in these two paragraphs.

Also unusual in the narrative style is the fact that he is clearly alert, not given

**Narration**

to be over-trusting: he takes precautions to check when first offered the job ('Ah, smart, smart!', cries 'Arthur Pinner') and sees through the disguise himself by means of the gold tooth. He even organises Holmes and Watson to an extent, making up identities and reasons for visiting the offices. Hall Pycroft prides himself on his sharpness and exclaims in horror, 'What a blind beetle I have been!'. Maybe so, but also one of the most engaging and energetic of Holmes' clients!

---

**Examiner's tip**

There are many ways of adding variety to what might seem a set formula. In narrative *The Stockbroker's Clerk* follows a fairly typical pattern (unexpected suicide attempt apart), but the character of Hall Pycroft re-defines the role of victim in ebullient style.

---

## Deception unmasked

The final drama is based on coincidence: 'Pinner' buys a newspaper just

**Deception**

before the three arrive at his office; this prompts his actions which reveal the full extent of the crime. However, the real detective work is not to do with the actual robbery and murder, but with impersonation, a common theme in Holmes stories. The key moment is when Holmes asks himself what special qualities Pycroft has to make his services so valuable.

The answer, of course, is none, except as an employee of Mawson's whom no one would recognise. This is by no means the only story in which the focus of the client's attention is quite different from the focus of the criminal's. Pycroft wonders what is going on in Birmingham; nothing, in fact, is going on, except that he is being detained there by peaceful means. You should be able to think of another story in which high pay for meaningless tasks is simply a decoy.

# The 'Gloria Scott'

*Holmes shows Watson a letter which is a memento of his first case. Whilst at college, he develops his system of observation without having any idea that it can be used to make a living. On going to stay with his only friend, Victor Trevor, he impresses Mr Trevor, senior, with his observations before causing him to faint at Holmes' deductions about the initials 'J.A.'. The story unfolds with the visit of a seaman, Hudson, who* is clearly blackmailing Trevor, Hudson's departure to stay with Beddoes, an old friend of Trevor's, and Trevor's fatal stroke on receiving the nonsensical letter from Beddoes. Holmes breaks the code: Hudson has told the police. All that remains is for young Trevor to find his father's account of his early years: real name James Armitage, sentenced to transportation for theft, involvement in Jack Prendergast's mutiny aboard the 'Gloria Scott', escape before the destruction of the ship. Armitage and his friend, Evans, rescued Hudson from the wreckage and now, as Trevor and Beddoes, respectable land-owners, are subject to his blackmail. What finally happens to Beddoes and Hudson is a mystery.

## Young Sherlock Holmes

Narration

The narrative method is totally different from most Holmes stories. Dr Watson is not involved, except as audience, and Sherlock Holmes is not engaged as a detective in any conventional way. True, he solves the mystery of the note, but the true unravelling of the mystery comes in Mr Trevor's own account. What is interesting is the portrait of the young Holmes.

Holmes' solitary habits are described as having been fixed even at college: he spends the next seven weeks of the vacation 'working out a few

Sherlock Holmes

experiments in organic chemistry'. He is more interested in 'working out my own little methods of thought' than in socialising or conventional study. He gains a friend only from the unlikely occurrence of being attacked by his bull-terrier! His 'habits of observation and inference', as shown by his analysis of Mr Trevor, are already well developed, and for the first time he receives the idea that they might provide him with a profession.

## Two tales in one

As a detective story The 'Gloria Scott' is somewhat unsatisfactory. Most of the stories contain extended narratives from victims, criminals or newspapers, but these become an integral part of Holmes' investigations. In this case the nature of the crime is obvious (Trevor has a past from his days at sea or in the gold mines, Hudson is blackmailing him) before very nearly half of the story is devoted to a tale of bloody deeds on the high seas. A final paragraph, then, is inconclusive.

Danger

You should be able to relate The 'Gloria Scott' to certain recurring themes and subjects in the Holmes stories: respectable landowner with a past, for instance, but particularly the dangers and opportunities of the colonies. Remember that Australia for much of the nineteenth century was both the site of a penal colony and a land of opportunity for material success.

# The Musgrave Ritual

*Sherlock Holmes recalls another early case of his. Reginald Musgrave, a university acquaintance, lives at Hurlstone, an ancient manor house in Sussex, where two of the staff have recently disappeared. Brunton, the excellent butler, was found in the library at night going through papers, comparing the text of the Musgrave Ritual with a chart. Musgrave gave him a week's notice. Two days later he disappeared. Rachel Howells, the housemaid whom he had loved and then betrayed, became hysterical and two days later ran away, her prints leading to the lake. Dragging for her body, Musgrave found a bag containing old discoloured metal. On reading the Musgrave Ritual, an apparently meaningless catechism given to all Musgraves when they reach manhood, Holmes realises that it contains the solution to the mystery. Following the clues, as Brunton did before him, he finds the dead butler in a small chamber beneath the cellar. Perhaps Rachel closed the lid on him; perhaps it was an accident. Re-examining the Ritual, Holmes realises that the old metal found in the lake (thrown away by Rachel after Brunton found it) is the ancient crown of the Kings of England, hidden for the deposed Stuarts.*

## A difficult room-mate

Again Sherlock Holmes recounts one of his early cases, but Dr Watson has a more interesting role than in *The 'Gloria Scott'*. The opening is set in the days before Watson's marriage, when they are fellow-lodgers in Baker Street, and Watson's descriptions and his exchanges with Holmes bring out the eccentricity and humour of his character. The opening paragraph vividly captures the wilful chaos of Holmes' domestic life: surely we are to see decorating the wall with 'a patriotic V.R. (Victoria Regina – Queen Victoria) done in bullet-pocks' as amusing rather than violent.

It is also amusing to find the great detective gently reproved into tidying his room and mischievously distracting Watson by the promise of a good story. The presentation of evidence ('a crumpled piece of paper, an old-fashioned brass key, a peg of wood with a ball of string attached to it and three rusty old discs of metal') serves to whet the appetite.

## History

It is evident that Conan Doyle looked for variety in the Sherlock Holmes stories by departing from the conventional detective story from time to time. Sherlock Holmes here solves a mystery, though without being able to establish whether murder has been done, but the interest lies equally with the historical element of the story.

Though the events are fictional, historically the story is convincing enough. The overthrow of Charles I and the House of Stuart forced the future Charles II to escape to the Continent: who knows what might have been hidden with sympathisers? Make a list of details that create a sense of history and mystery combined, beginning with Holmes' first description of Musgrave, a man with the air of belonging to 'perhaps the oldest inhabited building in the county'.

## The first of the master-criminals?

Though not, one imagines, a habitual criminal, Brunton, the butler, is in a sense the earliest of Holmes' master-criminals. Holmes respects the criminals whose boldness, intelligence and logical powers make them worthy opponents. Brunton's strengths and weaknesses are summed up by Musgrave early in the story: he has 'personal advantages and extraordinary gifts', but 'he is a bit of a Don Juan' (a fickle lover of great sexual appetite).

The criminals

So his extraordinary gifts lead him to the treasure; his Don Juan tendencies cause his death. Sherlock Holmes pays tribute to him several times: the comment on the comparative intelligence of Brunton and 'ten generations of his masters' fits well with some of Holmes' disparaging comments about the aristocracy in other stories.

## Deduction and imagination

As Holmes points out in *Silver Blaze*, imagination is the key, though all imaginative hypotheses have to be tested by evidence. The early signs of detective skills show in his realising that the secret of the disappearances lies in the Musgrave Ritual, not the only case of a key message being conveyed in apparently meaningless form.

Deduction

# The Reigate Squires

*Sherlock Holmes, suffering from nervous exhaustion after a particularly trying case, goes with Watson to stay with Colonel Hayter near Reigate. He hears of a robbery at the house of a local magnate, Acton, in which a very odd selection of items was stolen. The* next morning comes news of the murder of William, the coachman, at the house of the Cunninghams, bitter rivals of Acton in a land dispute – clearly the same gang! Holmes, asked for his advice by the local inspector, is fascinated by a torn-off scrap of paper in the dead man's hand, giving the time of the murder. Enthused by the case, he goes to the Cunninghams' and soon after sends for Watson and the Colonel. Using a series of pretexts, he builds the case against the Cunninghams to the extent that they attack him and are arrested. Holmes explains his detailed reasoning and also what old Cunningham has now revealed. The Cunninghams tried to steal a crucial document from Acton, then faked a robbery; William knew of it and attempted blackmail, so the Cunninghams lured him to the house and killed him, using the robbery fears as a cover-up.

## A virtuoso performance

This is vintage Holmes, both in deductive powers and in theatrical presentation. It is also vintage Conan Doyle in narrative style. The opening three paragraphs are, of course, a pretext to get Holmes to Reigate, but more importantly a triumphant fanfare for the world's greatest detective and a ready excuse for some of his most gloriously eccentric behaviour. It is a common device for Conan Doyle to refer casually to major cases when Holmes is solving an apparently lesser mystery, but never is it done more effectively than here. Examine the adjectives used to create an impression of huge achievement and reputation, plus physical and emotional anguish; in particular, savour the use of proper names to give a convincing international flavour to the proceedings.

Narration

### Contrast: procedurals

This story sees Sherlock Holmes at the opposite extreme from the procedurals: crime is a holiday task, not a daily routine; he is at his most amateur: 'I'll tell you what! I should like to have a quiet little glance ... '; the sense of performing to an audience is inescapable.

Sherlock Holmes

Consider how his illness enables Holmes to deceive friends and criminals alike. Make a list of instances where Holmes behaves oddly or Watson feels worried about his health: all are for a purpose.

The man's obsession with investigation and detection is neatly summed up in the last sentence: worn down by his efforts, he has gone to Reigate for a rest, solved two crimes and been assaulted by two men, as a result of which he feels sufficiently invigorated to resume his practice!

## A case of logic

This is a logically complete piece of deduction. Some of the flaws he exposes

Deduction

in the Cunninghams' story are actually fairly obvious: the repeat burglary theory is none too likely. Why is it that the inspector (no fool, this time) cannot see this? Other elements of the investigation are masterly, in particular, the deductions from the letter: written by two people (to divide guilt), one younger and stronger-willed laying down the template for the other to fill in, family resemblance, plus the 'twenty three other deductions' that he adds as a last flourish.

Deception

The ingenuity and cunning of the investigation are equally important: ill-health is used as a constant deception and his supposedly failing powers not only inspire self-confident mockery from Alec, but secure a handwriting sample from his

father. Before the meticulous explanation, there is the bravura performance of solving the crime in one visit, complete with fits and fisticuffs.

## Holmes and the police

Inspector Forrester is presented in fairly favourable terms. Described as 'a

The police

smart, keen-faced young fellow', he summarises the evidence intelligently, and his theory that William Kirwan was in league with the burglar is greeted with unusual approval from Holmes: 'an ingenious and not entirely an impossible supposition.' Can you suggests how far Holmes' generosity of feeling towards the inspector is explained by the inspector's manner towards Holmes? However, the police and Holmes

take very different views of investigations. Worried by Holmes' odd behaviour and the possibility of illness, Forrester is reassured by Watson that there is method in his madness. 'Some folk might say there was madness in his method,' is the Inspector's muttered reply, speaking for policemen everywhere.

# ■ Self-test questions – *Silver Blaze* to *The Reigate Squires*

**Who? What? When? Where? How? Why?**

1  Who organised the mutiny on the Gloria Scott?
2  Who was John Hebron of Atlanta, Georgia?
3  Who is Holmes' host at Reigate?
4  Who owns the second favourite for the Wessex Cup?

5   Who is Janet Tregellis?
6   What task is Hall Pycroft given in Birmingham?
7   What is the real name of Mr Beddoes?
8   When did the Musgrave Ritual originate?
9   Where is Silver Blaze found?
10   Where is Holmes lying ill after his exertions in the Spring of 1887?
11   How did John Straker conceal the taste of powdered opium when drugging the stable lad?
12   How does Holmes cause Mr Trevor to faint?
13   How does Holmes secure a sample of old Mr Cunningham's writing?
14   Why does Holmes tell Watson the tale of the Musgrave Ritual?
15   Why did the Cunninghams commit the robbery at Mr Acton's house?

## Important clues
What is the significance of the following clues, either in solving crimes or in demonstrating Holmes' expertise?
1   The lameness of the sheep
2   Mr Trevor's flat thick ears
3   The word 'quarter' written in a squeezed up manner
4   Pipe tobacco, Grosvenor mixture, at eightpence an ounce
5   Prints from a horse and a man reversing direction
6   A gold filling
7   A bill for 37 pounds, 15 shillings, from Madame Lesurier of Bond Street
8   A letter accepting employment with the Franco-Midland Hardware Company, Ltd.?
9   Strong 't's and weaker 't's
10   A spent match found in the mud

## Who said this about what or whom?
1   'That was the curious incident.'
2   'You don't seem to be so very quick after all.'
3   'That's your way of life, sir, and you may take the word of a man who has seen something of the world.'
4   ' ... a nobler man never walked the earth.'
5   '... the real murderer is standing immediately behind you!'

## Follow the theme
When Conan Doyle was writing these stories which, of course, originally appeared in magazines, Sherlock Holmes was already one of the most famous and established characters in fiction. Bearing this in mind, compare these six stories in terms of:
a)   the effectiveness of their opening sections;
b)   the reasons why Holmes becomes involved in the investigations;
c)   the attempts to present Holmes' character in different ways.

# The Crooked Man

*Colonel James Barclay has apparently been murdered in Aldershot. The colonel, who had risen through the ranks, was a devoted husband and a jovial character, but with strange moments of violence and depression. On the return of his wife from a Guild* meeting, they were heard having a furious quarrel in a locked room. By the time the coachman entered through the French window, the Colonel was dead in a pool of his own blood and his wife insensible with shock. Investigations reveal (among other evidence) signs of a strange animal who appears to have entered with the likely murderer. Holmes has persuaded Miss Morrison, Mrs Barclay's companion at the Guild, to tell the truth, which is that they met a cripple on the way back whom Mrs Barclay knew from years before. Holmes takes Watson with him to see this cripple, Henry Wood, who tells a tale of rivals in love in the Indian Army, Barclay's betrayal of him to his supposed death and Barclay's collapse at sight of him. The strange creature is a mongoose, the inquest verdict is apoplexy.

## A tale of Empire

This is not only a detective story, but an army romance, a tale of the mysterious east and a morality about sins of the past. Without Sherlock Holmes, but with more emphasis on the private lives and personalities of the Barclays and Henry Wood, you could imagine it succeeding as a tragic, rather melodramatic romance. It is complete with the trappings of a life in the Empire, from hand-carved club to mongoose, neither of which in fact has the sinister significance we expect.

Narration

Holmes serves as the link to draw out the sad story. Proceeding logically from Mrs Barclay's earlier behaviour (quite normal) to her conduct on return (disturbed) to the violent quarrel (highly unusual), he concludes that the answer to the problem lies in the hour and a half she was away, and puts pressure on Miss Morrison. Having heard her story, he is in a position to find Henry Wood and hear his. Thus the saga of love, betrayal, return and death can unfold.

## Intimations of evil

Holmes' investigations impress the reader with the mystery and potential for evil in a totally non-criminal case in which the most reprehensible conduct was that of the dead man over thirty years previously. The story is full of false trails of evidence which convince us that the tale is more complicated and evil than it really is.

Deduction

Consider the part played in Holmes' investigations by the following and write down the truth about each:

- the mysterious creature;
- the hard-carved club;
- the missing key;
- the contorted face;
- the name 'David' (the relevant Biblical reference is explained below).

## All are victims

In this story all three central characters are seen as victims: both of the Barclays and Henry Wood. All are presented sympathetically, even Colonel Barclay

*The victims*

who was a popular leader of men and whose depressions clearly show his sense of guilt. His great sin, betraying his colleague through jealous love of the same girl, is no worse than that of the great King David as told in the Second Book of Samuel, Chapter 11. David committed adultery with Bathsheba, wife of Uriah the Hittite. David ordered Uriah to be placed in 'the forefront of the hottest battle' where 'he may be smitten and die'. Uriah was killed; David and Bathsheba were married.

# The Resident Patient

*Dr Trevelyan, an accomplished doctor without funds, was assisted by an odd man by the name of Blessington who set him up in Brook Street, paid all bills, installed himself upstairs as resident patient and took his daily share of the proceeds. Dr Trevelyan comes to Holmes as a result of events which have shattered Blessington's nerve. He has been severely panicked by reading of a robbery, then a Russian nobleman and his son have paid two visits to the surgery. They have acted mysteriously and, on the second occasion, the son has clearly entered Blessington's room. Holmes finds a terrified Blessington in fear of his life, but he refuses to tell the truth and Holmes leaves. The next morning comes news of Blessington's suicide by hanging, which Holmes proves to be murder with the aid of such clues as footprints, scratches by the lock and cigar butts. By checking at headquarters Holmes finds that the murderers are members of the Worthingdon bank gang, and Blessington was Sutton, 'the worst of the gang', who informed on the others: they have gained their revenge on release from prison.*

## Rough justice

*The criminals*

The tendency of Holmes to dismiss the uncooperative can be disturbing at times, and we may doubt the compassion of a man who leaves Blessington in fear of his life simply because he is lying and unhelpful. However, popular Victorian literature was often less tolerant of the 'undeserving' (and more inclined to sentimentalise the 'deserving') than we are today. These are crooks: they get what they deserve. Read the paragraph about 'the dreadful sight' and see if you think that there is an element of ghoulish enjoyment in it: Conan Doyle seems happy to apply a harsh morality to Sutton/Blessington. As for the others, the page-boy is unimportant, a non-character whose opening of the door to the murderers makes the suicide theory possible. Biddle, Hayward and Moffat suffer a form of rough justice Conan Doyle has employed before: they are drowned when their ship sinks.

## A bizarre tale

Unlike some of the other stories, the reader feels little sympathy for anyone here. The appeal of the story is in its gallery of evil grotesques and two *tours de force* of deduction by Holmes.

The first is probably the more impressive. Many stories begin with a display

Deduction

of Holmes' powers of observation and interpretation, but this is different: reading Watson's thoughts from his expressions. As so often with Holmes, the explanation comes later: Watson's first hint of what is going on is when Holmes interrupts his thoughts by agreeing with them! The second is the final proof of the murder, a meticulous and convincing analysis of evidence, though the final unmasking of the criminals takes a less than convincing form.

The police

How, one asks oneself, could the Inspector have so little idea of how to work out the identity of the murderers when they are 'well-known at headquarters'? However, the police at least secure the erring page-boy with some speed, though the 'lack of evidence' at his court appearance again suggests the incompetence that seems to beset the police in the presence of Sherlock Holmes.

# The Greek Interpreter

*Sherlock Holmes and Watson visit Sherlock's brother, Mycroft, at the Diogenes Club. Mycroft introduces them to Mr Melas, a Greek interpreter who lodges on the floor above him. Mr Melas tells of being taken by a young man, Latimer, to a secret destination where he is forced to question, in Greek, an emaciated prisoner about whether he will consent to sign some papers. By cunning Melas finds out that he is called Kratides, is from Athens and has been a prisoner for three weeks. At this point a woman appears and each calls the other's name: 'Paul!' 'Sophy!' before both are dragged away and Melas removed. Mycroft and Melas have taken some steps to advertise for information about Paul Kratides. The case is so clear that Watson works it out: a rich Greek lady is abducted by Latimer, her brother comes to rescue her and is captured. A reply to Mycroft's advertisement arrives and the action is stepped up: Melas is taken by Paul's captors and Holmes, Watson and Inspector Gregson head for the address in Beckenham given by their informant. When they arrive, Latimer and his accomplice, Wilson Kemp, have fled with Sophy, leaving Melas and Kratides to die of charcoal poisoning. Help is too late for Kratides; Melas survives.*

## Abduction, evil and a little mystery

The answer to the mystery is easily found by advertising and receiving an instant reply from J. Davenport of Lower Brixton. The reason why the Greek is held prisoner is so straightforward that Watson summarises with the merest details corrected by Holmes.

Dr Watson

Watson, we may feel, is more astute than he appears next to Holmes, but he is hardly an investigator of note and usually plays the role of the onlooker who sees, but does not observe. So there is not really a mystery for Holmes to solve, and his contribution to the plot consists of warnings to Melas, mobilising Gregson, and skill in breaking and entering and identifying charcoal.

The criminals

There are some good moments of excitement, notably Melas' questioning of Kratides and the race to The Myrtles to save Kratides and Melas, but the ending is unsatisfactory: yet another example of rough justice where escaped criminals get their just deserts in some distant place.

## Characters

The appeal of the story rests mainly in the characters, not particularly Sophy

The victims

and Paul or the captors, though the giggling Kemp with his mesmeric effect on Melas is a colourful villain. Melas is an engaging victim, chatty, vivid in his account, inventive and totally devoid of physical courage, touchingly upset by the police's disregard for 'my poor man with the sticking-plaster upon his face'.

The major enjoyment of the story is the appearance of Mycroft Holmes, so shy of society that Watson has never heard of his existence before now: his visit to Baker Street with news of an answer to the advertisement is a unique event that he enjoys with innocent self-satisfaction.

---

**Examiner's tip**

Mycroft Holmes is undoubtedly the most inspired creation in these stories apart from the two central characters. The novelty of an investigation instigated by a man completely without energy is amusing, but also serves to emphasise that Sherlock Holmes is a man of action, as well as a perfect machine for thinking.

---

Mycroft Holmes possesses his brother's powers of observation and deduction to a superior degree, but is too lazy to do anything. He has helped to found the Diogenes Club for people like himself who dislike society, and his routine is absurdly unchanging: a quarter to five till twenty to eight at the Diogenes every evening. (Diogenes, incidentally, was an Ancient Greek philosopher with a low opinion of his fellow men who lived a solitary life in a tub!) The exchange between the Holmes brothers in the bow-window of the club is an amusing display of competitive deduction.

Deduction

Like comedians capping each other's punch-lines, they compete in finding ever more obscure information about the passing populace. Mycroft himself says, 'Sherlock has all the energy of the family', but after all it is a response to Mycroft's entry in the *Daily News*, not Sherlock's energetic idea of wiring the Athens police, that reveals the whereabouts of Paul Kratides.

# The Naval Treaty

*Watson receives a letter from an old school friend, Percy Phelps who, by ability and an influential uncle, has gained a post in the Foreign Office, but who is now likely to lose it because of a disaster that occurred nine weeks previously, since when he has been sick with brain fever. Holmes and Watson visit him at his house, Briarbrae: he is nursed by his fiancée, Annie Harrison, and her brother Joseph is also in residence. Phelps lost a secret naval treaty, stolen from his office at night while he was copying it. Whilst he was speaking to the commissionaire, the bell from his office rang, then the treaty was found to be missing. Evidence abounds, including the suspicious behaviour of the commissionaire's wife. On his second visit to Phelps Holmes is informed that someone tried to break into his bedroom the previous night, the first night there was no nurse in his room. Holmes sets a trap: Annie sits in Phelps' bedroom all day and he takes Phelps to Baker Street. However, Holmes returns to Briarbrae and lies in wait for Joseph Harrison, who attempts to retrieve the treaty from beneath the floor of what was previously his bedroom. Holmes is able to give Phelps the treaty and an explanation over breakfast in Baker Street.*

## A complicated investigation

'The principal difficulty in your case,' Holmes tells Percy Phelps, 'lay in the

Deduction

fact of there being too much evidence.' Holmes' investigative powers in this story (nearly twice as long as most stories in the *Memoirs*) depend not on finding evidence, but on deciding what to discard. The story is a variant on the 'locked room' plot: there are two entrances, but Phelps himself occupied the main entrance. Therefore the criminal is someone who knows the lay-out of the offices, but why should he draw attention

The criminals

to himself by ringing the bell? The obvious assumption is that a crime of this international importance was planned well in advance. It is only by removing this preconception that Holmes can unmask the opportunist criminal who seized his chance, having already rung for attention.

The placing of suspicion on innocent people is handled with some subtlety: throughout there are several valid suspects. In the interview with Forbes at Scotland Yard, Holmes questions him in detail about the commissionaire's wife, Mrs Tangey, and concludes, 'She has at least an answer for everything': innocent of the crime or simply plausible? The interview with Lord Holdhurst throws up two suspects, each in fact innocent, though Lord Holdhurst's hint at Phelps himself ('An attack of brain fever, for example?') has an element of truth in it. Write down the reasons for and against Mrs Tangey and Lord Holdhurst as suspects.

## Reliable witnesses

The reason why Sherlock Holmes has such a mass of accumulated evidence to sift is that he can call upon the testimony of reliable and intelligent people who have had nine weeks to consider the case. Approximately half the story consists of interviews with Phelps, Forbes and Lord Holdhurst, all frank and well informed. Of assistance to Holmes is that the treaty will not remain secret much longer, so that the criminal must make his profit soon. The coincidence of Phelps feeling well enough to sleep alone in the room drives Harrison to precipitate action and thus Holmes is able to bait the trap.

Deception

Holmes' delight in deception surfaces here, although he does not resort to elaborate disguise, merely deception of even Watson as to his whereabouts, culminating in the presentation of the treaty to Phelps at breakfast.

'I never can resist a touch of the dramatic,' says Holmes, rather in contrast to his claims elsewhere to be purely scientific and opposed to Watson's sensationalised narratives. The actual investigation has depended on isolating what is important. How do you establish a pattern when Mrs Tangey's fearful reaction to 'two men in the house' proves unimportant, but Phelps' change of bedroom and nine weeks of attended illness are crucial?

Sherlock Holmes

## Victorian London

London

As ever with the stories set in London, whether in seedy dockland, the clubland of Pall Mall or the Foreign Office, the topography is thoroughly convincing. Methods of transport, too, always seem meticulously researched: one can imagine Conan Doyle having to hand a railway timetable, an

Underground map and a scale of charges for hansom cabs. All this is apparent in *The Naval Treaty*, as is a close knowledge of the growing suburbia of not-quite-country houses. What is remarkable, though, is Holmes' vision of the future amid the terraces of Clapham. The Board schools, products of the 1870 Education Act, are 'beacons of the future': the great man clearly has a social conscience!

# The Final Problem

*Sherlock Holmes arrives at Watson's consulting room after a long spell in France. He is clearly on the run and explains that behind much of the major crime in London is the evil genius Professor Moriarty. Holmes has collected sufficient evidence for the arrest of the Professor, but it is necessary to wait till the following Monday for the police to act. In the meantime Moriarty has visited Baker Street to threaten Holmes and made many attempts, disguised as accidents, to kill him. Holmes proposes to Watson that they should go abroad until the arrest is made. With difficulty they escape from London and travel towards Switzerland. Holmes learns that, although the rest of the gang has been arrested, Moriarty has escaped. Holmes is quite willing to sacrifice his own life to end the career of the Napoleon of Crime and, when Watson is lured away from the Reichenbach Falls and both Holmes and Moriarty apparently fall to their deaths in a fatal struggle, it seems that this has happened.*

### Is it the final problem?

This story is marked by Conan Doyle's desire to rid himself of his most popular character, whose success distracted the author and his public from his more serious work. Having said this, it is noticeable that, in the way of soap opera plot-lines, he leaves a possibility of resurrection: Sherlock Holmes' body is not found. In other ways it is obvious that Conan Doyle is seeking a dramatic finale.

Danger

Never previously was Holmes in so much danger. The very streets of London seem engaged in the attempt to kill him: even 221B Baker Street is fired. The tentacles of the master-criminal stretch from special trains instantly engaged to Swiss youths in Moriarty's service. The theme of great moral good is stressed: Holmes has often looked for cases that engage his intelligence and interest: the social good is secondary. Now he talks nobly of 'the air of London' being 'sweeter for my presence'.

### 'The Napoleon of crime'

Danger

Moriarty is the personification of the evil genius: read the account of his career early in the story or the description of his personal appearance when he visits Holmes. There is a note of generosity in Holmes' last letter, a sense of worthy opponents fighting a duel, but Conan Doyle is too wise to glamorise him generally: he is evil and must be removed, by prison or death.

**Detective stories**

The evil genius of crime has become a stock figure, but Moriarty remains the most famous of the breed. Why? The inspired choice of name and nickname ('The Napoleon of crime') helps, but above all the mix of mystery and evil ('The man pervades London and no one has heard of him.').

It is perhaps disappointing that we have no details of his crimes, except against Holmes, or how he was detected, but the story is of pursuit and confrontation, not, for once, detection and investigation: Holmes' deductive powers are applied solely to eluding Moriarty. In many ways this is far from the best of the Holmes stories, but it contains many memorable images, notably in the final pages. We know from the opening how the story will end (Watson defending his friend against the accusations of Colonel Moriarty is an excellent pretext for the story) and the tension builds, not only via ominous events, but also the graphic intensity of the descriptions. Before the final farewell and tribute, it is highly appropriate to find Dr Watson trying, not without success, to apply Holmes' own methods: by no means the first case where footprints have provided crucial evidence!

# ■ Self-test questions – *The Crooked Man* to *The Final Problem*

**Who? What? When? Where? How? Why?**

1  Who are Biddle, Hayward and Moffat?
2  Who pays off the brokers with her husband's pension?
3  Who defends his brother by letters in the press?
4  Who was nicknamed 'Tadpole'?
5  Who was 'the smartest man in the 117th Foot'?
6  What has prints like a dog and climbs curtains?
7  What disguise does Holmes assume at Victoria when escaping from Moriarty?
8  When does Holmes return the treaty to Phelps?
9  When did Mycroft Holmes think that Sherlock would be out of his depth?
10  Where is the Naval Treaty found?
11  Where does it appear that Latimer and Kemp die?
12  How does Moriarty decoy Watson away from Holmes?
13  How does Colonel Barclay die?
14  Why did Dr Percy Trevelyan become involved with Mr Blessington?
15  Why does Henry Wood settle in Aldershot?

**Important clues**

What is the significance of the following clues, either in solving crimes or in demonstrating Holmes' expertise?

1 Four cigar ends
2 A man wearing his 'ammunition boots'
3 Re-soled boots
4 An attempt to break into Phelps' bedroom
5 The repeated word 'David'
6 Ringing the bell in the office
7 A screwdriver and four screws
8 Watson's used, but not dirty, boots

**Who said this about what or whom?**

1 'I will never so much as breathe the same air as you again! You coward!'
2 'It does seem a very preposterous way of settling a dispute.'
3 'Lighthouses, my boy! Beacons of the future!'
4 'You have less frontal development than I should have expected.'
5 'I was quite convinced that ... was a hoax.'
6 '... is the queerest club in London and ... one of the queerest men.'
7 'It is a very easy complaint to imitate. I have done it myself.'
8 'If you fail me, then my honour as well as my position are for ever forfeited.'

**Follow the theme**

Follow the theme of crime and punishment through all 11 stories in the Memoirs. Consider what crimes are committed, how the criminals are punished and whether the punishments are appropriate. You should examine how many are punished by the law and how many outside the law.

# How to write a coursework essay

Most of you are probably studying Sherlock Holmes stories as part of a Wide Reading coursework assignment for GCSE English/English Literature. If we look at the requirement of the NEAB examinations, we find that this assignment must involve *comparison* between a complete pre-twentieth-century prose text and at least one suitable twentieth-century text. It is also essential to make certain comments on the historical, social and cultural background to the texts. One of the suggestions of the NEAB syllabus is a consideration of the genre of the detective story as used by Conan Doyle and one or more twentieth-century writer(s). This is a promising subject, not least for the way it satisfies the historical/cultural requirement: the contemporary setting is of great importance in any detective story, and the whole culture of the genre is founded on Sherlock Holmes. In the following pages we examine some possible approaches. Throughout the **Text commentary** the **Essays icon** draws attention to useful material for your assignment.

There are, of course, some general principles for these assignments.

*Comparison is essential.* No credit is given for telling the story of a Sherlock Holmes mystery followed by the story of a Colin Dexter novel. It is essential that you show that, while Conan Doyle presents his mysteries in a certain way, your twentieth-century author does it in the same way, similarly or totally differently.

There is no requirement that your twentieth-century comparison is prose fiction: as well as short stories and novels, plays are acceptable, though not normally television detective serials. The only restriction is that the text 'must be of sufficient substance and quality to merit serious study' – a difficult point to decide in detective fiction. There are some crime novelettes that are clearly unsuitable; Colin Dexter and Ruth Rendell would probably be acceptable, but Agatha Christie is probably best avoided.

Your choice of twentieth-century text(s) is important. There must be *specific* grounds for comparison. If you choose a detective story/novel, these grounds are obvious. If you choose another sort of crime novel or thriller, you need to be careful to establish these grounds for comparison, although you should remember that creating an opposite effect can also make for valid comparison. You should note that there are many Sherlock Holmes stories written in the twentieth century by other writers: you can use these if you and your teacher feel that the writing is of sufficient quality.

The *most important* consideration in writing the essay is that it must develop an argument or explain a point of view consistently throughout. The comparison should be made *throughout* the essay, not necessarily in the same sentence, but at least in adjacent paragraphs. Careful advance planning will aid you in organising your theme or argument: making notes on the material, putting these notes in order, then working through two or three drafts of the essay. Thus you should be able to make a decision on what each paragraph is about, as far as possible signalling that to the reader in the opening sentence, often called a *topic sentence* because it states the topic of the paragraph.

In terms of length of essay, do bear in mind that it is only one of several pieces of coursework and there is no need for a 5,000 word blockbuster. Many essays will exceed 1,000 words: by how much depends on the material you wish to present and the advice of your teacher.

## Detective stories: the genre

*What do you consider to be the main qualities of the detective story as a genre? Compare the Sherlock Holmes stories with one or more twentieth-century example.*

There were detective stories before Conan Doyle. *The Woman in White* (1860) by Wilkie Collins is generally regarded as the first novel to deal with the detection of crime. It was, however, the Sherlock Holmes stories that established the first vogue for detective fiction and influenced beyond measure the vast growth in such stories in the twentieth-century. The choice, therefore, of comparisons is enormous: you must make your own choice. It is not essential, but you will produce a better essay by referring to more than one Holmes story (not all 23 in this guide, of course, maybe three or four) and, if possible, two or more twentieth-century authors.

Conan Doyle established the detective as a loner, working outside the system, though often with a loyal, less eccentric assistant. In the American classic, *The Maltese Falcon*, by Dashiell Hammett, Sam Spade's uneasy relationship with the police parallels Holmes'. The amateur detective in much English fiction, from G.K. Chesterton's Father Brown to Ellis Peters' Brother Cadfael, derives from Holmes' concern for the most interesting cases, not the most important. Though Holmes is paid, it is not his prime concern. Fictional detectives in the Police Force are seldom establishment figures. Chester Himes' Harlem detectives Coffin Ed Johnson and Grave Digger Jones cause as much trouble to their superiors as Inspector Morse (by Colin Dexter) whose assistant, Lewis is a perfect example of the sane and dutiful helper.

Sherlock Holmes established once and for all the pre-eminence of logic applied relentlessly, if unorthodoxly. Hercule Poirot's repeated babblings about the 'little grey cells' may irritate, but it sums up what the Holmes tradition is all about. Check the balance between chance and logic in your twentieth-century story(ies), and also the balance between thought and violence.

A convincing setting is all-important. There is a section in **Themes** on Holmes' London, and the authentic depiction of San Francisco (*The Maltese Falcon*) or Oxford (the Morse novels) is a major element in creating reader belief in what may be pretty unlikely stories. The historical detective stories (now very popular) use time instead of place in the same way.

You will probably find your twentieth-century example(s) offer more complicated plots than Conan Doyle's if you choose a novel rather than the refined simplicity of a 25-page story. It is likely, however, that you will identify similar elements. Miss Wonderly in distress entering Sam Spade's office at the start of *The Maltese Falcon* is pure Sherlock Holmes. You will identify the same need to distinguish between the incidental and the vital. Elements such as dramatic revelations of the truth, deceptions and disguises, 'red herrings' and doltish police may well still be present in the twentieth-century novel.

You might like to look at characterisation. If you are writing about a full-length novel, there should be fuller development of character among victims, suspects, etc., than in Sherlock Holmes stories. Holmes is ideally suited to the short story form because, even in his mellower version, he still has limited human sympathy: the problem at hand is his main interest. Compare your twentieth-century detective(s) in terms of human emotions.

Many stories in the English tradition share Conan Doyle's preference for the 'amateur' criminal, the person who is driven to crime by one or more of violent emotion (probably revenge), chance and greed. Gangs and professional criminals have a lower profile in the traditional English stories than in American novels. This, too, you can check in your comparison.

You will find many differences in detail in your twentieth-century comparison(s): less formality of speech and manners, more technology, probably more violence, etc. However, it is likely that you will find essential similarities in the presentation and solution of the case and the uniqueness/eccentricity/solitariness/deductive powers of the central character.

## A contrast: police procedurals and psychology

*Compare the approaches to crime and detection, and the presentation of criminals and the forces of law and order, in the Sherlock Holmes stories and Ed McBain's 87th Precinct novels.*

Reference to one Ed McBain novel would suffice, two or three would be admirable, but there is no point in suggesting titles here: the 87th Precinct novels, set in New York, are all very similar in approach and consistent in quality.

This is an essay that proceeds very much by way of contrasts. The 'procedural' is a novel which deals with the procedures and practices of the police rather than isolating one case. There is usually one central case to be solved in an 87th Precinct novel, but against a background of other cases and even such problems as the painters in the precinct office.

Similarly, there is not the concentration on one detective: there are something like sixteen officers in the precinct of different levels of brain-power, courage and astuteness. Private lives intrude to a greater extent than in Sherlock Holmes: Detective Steve Carella's wife is a character in the novels in a way that Mrs Watson never is in the short stories. The effect of this is a messier, more consistently violent, less logical, more realistic story. Authenticity of setting is an important factor in creating realism for both Conan Doyle and McBain.

You should be able, however, to find similarities. Conan Doyle was writing at a time when the quality of detective work had improved greatly over the previous 50 years. Thus he laid down a sort of template of detective techniques. Even in the 87th Precinct these still appear. So do the idea of the personal battle with the master-criminal (for Moriarty read the Deaf Man), use of disguise, eccentricity of both criminals and detectives, and a personal sense of humour (more rough-and-tumble in McBain, but very funny).

Another type of crime novel you could contrast with Sherlock Holmes is the type of thriller that uses the psychology of the criminal to grip the reader. Patricia Highsmith would be an excellent choice in this respect, either for the remarkable *Strangers on a Train* or the Ripley novels. Another fine crime novelist worth considering in these fields is Georges Simenon, both for the Maigret books (half-way between the lone detective and police procedural) and his psychological thrillers.

## The single story comparison: Roald Dahl

It is likely that some candidates will wish to make a comparison between a single Holmes story and a single modern story. This is quite acceptable within the examination guidelines. Roald Dahl's story, *Lamb to the Slaughter*, is a particularly popular choice.

The first thing to bear in mind is that, if you use only two stories of combined length of perhaps 50 pages, you need to compare them on every possible ground, so the title needs to ask for the comparison of the two as crime stories, their settings, characterisation and their appeal.

The first similarity is that *Lamb to the Slaughter* deals with murder; your Sherlock Holmes may well do, and almost certainly deals with some crime or violent death. Look for examples of ingenuity and the unexpected, though these are on the part of the criminal, not the detective, in the Dahl story.

Contrast the detectives: the humour of the ending of *Lamb to the Slaughter* comes from their destruction of the evidence. However, if the detectives are inept, the murderer is more thoroughly characterised.

Contrast narrative shape: the story of *Lamb to the Slaughter* is of the crime, the story of the Holmes tale is of the investigation.

You need to go into great detail on the difference in setting: not just the description of the modern world (a freezer is crucial to the story), but differences in manners, speech patterns, etc. This leads to a comparison of the actual style of writing (more formal in the Sherlock Holmes story) and of world-view (more cynical in Dahl's case). Only by such detailed examination can a single-story comparison produce a good assignment.

# How to write an examination essay

Though most of you will be required to write on the Sherlock Holmes stories as part of your coursework, some of you may need to answer an examination question on the *Adventures* or the *Memoirs*. This section considers one specific title on the stories, but also gives general advice on how to approach an English Literature examination essay.

*Analyse the ways in which Conan Doyle uses variety of plot, setting and mood to add interest to the stories in* The Adventures *(or* Memoirs*) of Sherlock Holmes.*

## Before you start writing

- The first essential is thorough revision. It is important that you realise that even Open Book examinations require close textual knowledge. You will have time to look up quotations and references, but *only if you know where to look.*

- Read the questions very carefully, both to choose the best one and to take note of exactly what you are asked to do.

- Do not answer the question you *imagine or hope* has been set. In the case of the title we are considering, there are three specific areas of variety to analyse. You must pay as much attention to the different settings (exotic settings in narratives of the past, as well as places from Dartmoor to the Reichenbach Falls) and mood (from logical contemplation to violent menace) as to the narratives. Remember also that discussing narrative variety does not mean telling the stories.

- Identify all the key words in the question that mention characters, events and themes, and instructions as to what to do, e.g. compare, contrast, comment, give an account, etc. In this case 'analyse' means identify the different parts and explain how they work, so you might explain how, in a story like *The Musgrave Ritual*, Conan Doyle uses a narrative technique that enables him to gain humour from the Holmes/Watson relationship while offering a different viewpoint (Holmes') on the character and story.

- Look at the points you have identified and jot down what you are going to say about each.

- Decide in what order you are going to deal with the main points. Number them in sequence. This is a matter of choice, but you should avoid a narrative approach: 'Holmes and Watson have to go to Dartmoor to investigate the disappearance of Silver Blaze.'

## Writing the essay

- The first sentences are important. Try to summarise your response to the question so the examiner has some idea of how you plan to approach it. For example: 'The classic format for a Sherlock Holmes story involves the arrival of a distraught stranger at Baker Street, an extended narrative from him/her, followed by an investigation of the scene of the crime by Holmes, the revelation of the truth and a final narrative/explanation from the detective. Though this is an excellent formula, Conan Doyle wisely uses variations on it to hold the reader's interest.' Jump straight into the essay; do not waste time at the start. A personal response is rewarded, but you must always answer the question – as you write your essay, *refer back* to your list of points.

- Answer *all* of the question. Many students spend all their time answering just one part of a question and ignoring the rest. This prevents you gaining marks for the parts left out. In the same way, failing to answer enough questions on the examination is a waste of marks which can always be gained most easily at the start of an answer.

- There is no 'correct' length for an essay. What you must do is spend the full time usefully in answering all parts of the question (spending longer than the allotted time by more than a few minutes is dangerous). Some people write faster than others; they don't always get the best marks! It is an advantage if you can organise your time well enough to reach an elegant conclusion (probably, in this case, a summary of your opinions or, rather more adventurously, an account of a story that succeeds by fitting the basic formula exactly), but it is better to leave an essay without a conclusion than to fail to start the next question.

- Take care with presentation, spelling and punctuation. It is generally unwise to use slang or contractions (e.g. 'they've' for 'they have').

- Use quotation or paraphrase when it is relevant and contributes to the quality and clarity of your answer. References to events often do not need quotation, but you would probably need the exact words of, for instance, one of Holmes' explanations of his methods. *Extended* quotations are usually unhelpful and are often used as padding, which is a complete waste of time.

# Answers to self-test questions – *A Scandal in Bohemia* to *The Man with the Twisted Lip*

## Who? What? When? Where? How? Why?

1 Jabez Wilson (*League*)
2 Colonel Openshaw (*Orange Pips*)
3 Irene Adler (*Bohemia*)
4 An old opium addict (Sherlock Holmes) (*Twisted Lip*)
5 The Red-Headed League
6 Ballarat in Australia (*Boscombe*)
7 Traveller for claret importers (*Identity*)
8 In Victoria, Australia (*Boscombe*)
9 Overnight in the St. Clairs' house in Kent (*Twisted Lip*)
10 Savannah, Georgia (*Orange Pips*)
11 In the cellar of a bank in the City of London (*League*)
12 'Stepping in at one door of a four-wheeler and out at the other' (*Identity*)
13 Mrs Watson offers sympathy and advice; Dr Watson rescues her addict husband (*Twisted Lip*)
14 Supposedly because of his aversion to Negroes; probably in some way he offended the Ku Klux Klan (*Orange Pips*)
15 He was (or thought he was) married (*Boscombe*)

## Important clues

1 They reveal Watson's muddy walk and incompetent servant. (*Bohemia*)
2 It gives him an excuse to spend time in the cellar digging a tunnel. (*League*)
3 It reveals that Neville St. Clair was in Hugh Boone's lodging (and at first suggests that he was murdered by Boone). (*Twisted Lip*)
4 It is 'a distinctly Australian cry' and reveals that McCarthy and Turner were together. (*Boscombe*)
5 The murderers are seamen: all are ports. (*Orange Pips*)
6 Young McCarthy is telling the truth and the murderer has a limp. (*Boscombe*)
7 'Hosmer Angel' disguised his speech. (*Identity*)
8 Mary Sutherland is a typist. (*Identity*)
9 The paper was made in Bohemia: 'Egria Papier Gesellschaft'. (*Bohemia*)
10 Neville St. Clair has no money problems, as his debts are only £88.10.0 (*Twisted Lip*)

## Who said this about what or whom?

1 Sherlock Holmes about the disguised Irene Adler (*Bohemia*)
2 Inspector Lestrade about the Boscombe Valley Mystery
3 Holmes about Watson (*Twisted Lip*)
4 Alice Turner about James McCarthy (*Boscombe*)
5 Colonel Openshaw about the arrival of the pips (*Orange Pips*)

## Follow the theme

1 In *Scandal in Bohemia* he specifically plans to break the law; in *The Boscombe Valley Mystery* he deliberately withholds information which would lead to the arrest of the murderer. He co-operates with the police to enforce the law only in *The Red-Headed League*. His contempt for the police shows in his treatment of Lestrade in *The Boscombe Valley Mystery* and in his furious comments in

*The Five Orange Pips*. His co-operation with the police (also in *The Man with the Twisted Lip*) depends upon their subservient position.

2   a)   *The Red-Headed League, The Boscombe Valley Mystery, The Five Orange Pips*

      b)   *A Scandal in Bohemia, The Boscombe Valley Mystery, The Five Orange Pips* (to some extent)

      c)   *The Red-Headed League*

None of these stories, therefore, deals with the simple plot of crime reported to Holmes – crime investigated and solved – criminal arrested.

# ■ Self-test answers – *The Blue Carbuncle* to *The Copper Beeches*

## Who? What? When? Where? How? Why?

1    James Ryder (*Carbuncle*)
2    Violet Hunter (*Beeches*)
3    Francis Prosper, Lucy Parr's sweetheart (*Coronet*)
4    Lord Backwater (*Bachelor*)
5    Excavating fuller's earth (*Thumb*)
6    A swamp adder
7    'The second morning after Christmas'
8    'Just two years ago' shortly before her marriage (*Band*)
9    In the gold mines of America (*Bachelor*)
10   At the receiver's who bought them from Sir George
11   By a skylight and a ladder with the assistance of Mr Fowler (*Beeches*)
12   By their initials: Flora Miller and Francis Hay Moulton (*Bachelor*)
13   Poisoned by a swamp adder wrapped around his head (*Band*)
14   Because she is too 'quiet and patient' to ask for her financial rights, but a husband would be more demanding (*Beeches*)
15   Because he is too frightened to do wrong again, to avoid him becoming a gaolbird, and because Horner is in no danger of conviction (*Carbuncle*)

## Important clues

1    The prices show it is a very select hotel and the Moultons can then be tracked down. (*Bachelor*)
2    It matches prints at Streatham, proving he received the coronet. (*Coronet*)
3    It indicates that Roylott wishes to communicate with his stepdaughter's room. (*Band*)
4    It is the first hint to Holmes that there was a ventilator. (*Band*)
5    It is proof of Henry Baker's decline from his previous foresight. (*Carbuncle*)
6    They show Arthur's pursuit of Sir George with signs of a scuffle in cut up snow and blood. (*Coronet*)
7    It is a ploy to exchange a note. (*Bachelor*)
8    It suggests that the house is nearer than Hatherley believes. (*Thumb*)
9    They are sounds associated with the return of the swamp-adder: the whistle summons the snake, then the safe closes on it. (*Band*)
10   It is proof that Roylott wants his victim in a set place. (*Band*)

## Who said this about what or whom?

1    Dr Grimesby Roylott about Sherlock Holmes (*Band*)

2 Sherlock Holmes ('laughing') about Lord St. Simon (*Bachelor*)
3 Breckenridge about his bet with Holmes on the origin of the goose (*Carbuncle*)
4 Hatherley about the hydraulic press (*Thumb*)
5 Holmes on Watson's narrative style (*Beeches*)

**Follow the theme**
1 Always these are troubled relationships, always the father is at fault, often the father is greedy for an inheritance. Dr Roylott (*Band*) and Jephro Rucastle (*Beeches*) seek to prevent a marriage by criminal means: in both these tales there is either a stepfather or stepmother. A similar relationship links Holder (*Coronet*) with his adoptive daughter: his problem is misjudging in different ways both her and his son. All these three seek to kill or imprison a son, daughter or stepdaughter. Aloysius Doran (*Bachelor*) is comparatively harmless, but he too places financial barriers in the way of his daughter's marriage.
2 a) Fritz as 'Colonel Stark', Ferguson as 'Dr Becher' (*Thumb*), Hatty Moulton as Lady St. Simon (innocent error) and Frank incognito (*Bachelor*), Violet Hunter (unknown to herself) as Alice (*Beeches*), Holmes as 'a loafer' (*Coronet*), James Ryder (briefly) as John Robinson (*Carbuncle*)
   b) *The Blue Carbuncle* and *The Noble Bachelor* take the reader on a chase through various parts of London, but the other four stories make use of isolation to make the crimes possible, as in Holmes' horror at the danger of the quiet countryside during the train journey in *The Copper Beeches*.

# ■ Self-test answers – *Silver Blaze* to *The Reigate Squires*

**Who? What? When? Where? How? Why?**
1 Jack Prendergast
2 First husband of Effie Munro (*Face*)
3 Colonel Hayter (*Squires*)
4 Lord Blackwater (*Blaze*)
5 Daughter of the head gamekeeper, 'taken up' with Brunton (*Musgrave*)
6 Marking off the hardware sellers in Paris from a directory (*Clerk*)
7 Evans (*Scott*)
8 In the middle of the seventeenth century, the time of the Civil War
9 At Capleton stables
10 The Hotel Dulong, Lyons (*Squires*)
11 Puts it in curried mutton (*Blaze*)
12 By drawing attention to his association with 'J.A.' (Trevor himself) (*Scott*)
13 By making an 'error' on the reward notice (*Squires*)
14 To avoid having to tidy his room
15 To secure a piece of paper essential to his claim on half their estate: it was not there and they stole various oddments to disguise their intentions (*Squires*)

**Important clues**
1 This shows that Straker practised laming the horse. (*Blaze*)
2 They prove that he used to be a boxer. (*Scott*)
3 It is proof that two people wrote the note and half the words were inserted in spaces. (*Squires*)

4   It shows that Grant Munro has 'no need to practise economy'. (*Face*)
5   They show that Silas Brown thought of returning Silver Blaze, but changed his mind.
6   Pycroft realised that the two Mr Pinners were one and the same. (*Clerk*)
7   This revealed Straker's extravagant double life. (*Blaze*)
8   It was needed as a sample of Pycroft's handwriting for his replacement to imitate. (*Clerk*)
9   These were the signs of the handwriting of the younger and older Cunninghams. (*Squires*)
10  It is proof that Straker used a light to help him nobble Silver Blaze.

**Who said this about what or whom?**
1   Sherlock Holmes about the failure of the dog to bark (*Blaze*)
2   Alec Cunningham about Holmes and his investigation (*Squires*)
3   Mr Trevor encouraging Holmes into a career as a detective (*Scott*)
4   Effie Munro about John Hebron (*Face*)
5   Holmes to Colonel Ross about Silver Blaze

**Follow the theme**
a)  Some take advantage of readers' knowledge by plunging immediately into dialogue: *Silver Blaze*, *The 'Gloria Scott'*. The stories are set at different times in the Holmes/Watson relationship, so sometimes Conan Doyle gives his readers a clue about where the story can be placed: *The Stockbroker's Clerk*, *The Reigate Squires*.
    Another device is for Watson to consider some aspect of Holmes' character as though giving the readers some new insight into a well-known character: *The Yellow Face*, *The Musgrave Ritual*.
b)  Generally he is called in by a client (Colonel Ross, Musgrave, Pycroft, Grant Munro), rarely the police (Inspector Forrester) . Note, however, the fact that he only responds to interesting cases: he ignored Ross at first. Note also the way in which mysteries pursue him by chance: his first case (*The 'Gloria Scott'*) or the invasion of his rest at Reigate.
c)  As in answer a), but notice also the way in which Conan Doyle tries to satisfy the need of the readers to see Holmes as real by including stories of his younger self. Notice also the variety of settings he is placed in: not too much London and 221B, Baker Street.

# ■ Self-test answers – *The Crooked Man* to *The Final Problem*

**Who? What? When? Where? How? Why?**
1   The Worthingdon bank gang, murderers of Blessington/Sutton (*Patient*)
2   Mrs Tangey (*Treaty*)
3   Colonel James Moriarty (*Problem*)
4   Percy Phelps when at school (*Treaty*)
5   Corporal Henry Wood (*Crooked Man*)
6   Teddy the mongoose (*Crooked Man*)
7   A venerable Italian priest (*Problem*)
8   Over breakfast at Baker Street (*Treaty*)
9   The previous week with the Manor House case (*Interpreter*)

10   Under the floor of Phelps' bedroom, previously Harrison's (*Treaty*)
11   Budapest (*Interpreter*)
12   By a false message about a dying English lady at the hotel (*Problem*)
13   Of apoplexy at the sight of Wood (*Crooked Man*)
14   He needed financial assistance to set up in private practice (*Patient*)
15   Longed for England and settled where the soldiers are to earn a living (*Crooked Man*)

## Important clues
1   This is proof of two men (different types of cigar) in Blessington's room. (*Patient*)
2   It is the sign of a man not long out of the service (used by Mycroft in detection competition with Sherlock). (*Interpreter*)
3   They show that Lord Holdhurst is short of money: something of a red herring. (*Treaty*)
4   It is a sign that the treaty is there. (*Treaty*)
5   It is Nancy's accusation of her husband's cruel removal of a rival in love: not understood at the time. (*Crooked Man*)
6   It shows that the theft was opportunist, not planned. (*Treaty*)
7   These show that Blessington's murderers were prepared for a hanging. (*Patient*)
8   They are proof that Watson is busy: he is using a hansom cab. (*Crooked Man*)

## Who said this about what or whom?
1   Mrs Barclay about her husband (*Crooked Man*)
2   Holmes about Watson's views on war, specifically the American Civil War, as observed and deduced by Holmes (*Patient*)
3   Holmes about Board Schools (*Treaty*)
4   Moriarty about Holmes (*Problem*)
5   Holmes in his letter to Watson about 'the letter from Meiringen' (*Problem*)
6   Holmes about the Diogenes Club and his brother Mycroft (*Interpreter*)
7   Holmes about a cataleptic fit (*Patient*)
8   Phelps about Holmes' search for the missing document (*Treaty*)

## Follow the theme
Surprisingly only 2 stories (*Stockbroker's Clerk/Reigate Squires*) see the main criminals arrested, though there are also the Moriarty gang (*Final Problem*) and the possibility of the arrest of Joseph in *The Naval Treaty*: it is not really in the interests of Holmes' clients to have a trial, so they are likely to escape. In some there is no crime to deal with: *Yellow Face*, *Crooked Man*, *Silver Blaze* (no major crime), *Musgrave Ritual* (maybe). Nearly everything is settled by rough justice, appropriate to the crime: John Straker (*Silver Blaze*), Trevor (rather harshly) and Hudson (probably) (*Gloria Scott*), Brunton (*Musgrave Ritual*), Barclay (*Crooked Man*), Blessington and the three drowned at sea (*Resident Patient*), Kemp and Latimer (*Greek Interpreter*) and Moriarty (*Final Problem*) . There remains, of course, Sherlock Holmes, but Conan Doyle's attempt to punish him for being too popular ultimately failed.

# Notes